# VIDEOTAPE ON TRIAL

———— **PEOPLE AND COMMUNICATION** ————

*Series Editors:* PETER CLARKE     *University of Michigan*
              F. GERALD KLINE     *University of Minnesota*

**Volumes in this series:**

# Gerald R. Miller
## and
# Norman E. Fontes

# VIDEOTAPE
# ON
# TRIAL
## A View from the Jury Box

 **SAGE Publications**    Beverly Hills    London

*For information address:*

**SAGE Publications, Inc.**
275 South Beverly Drive
Beverly Hills, California 90212

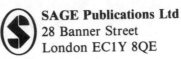

**SAGE Publications Ltd**
28 Banner Street
London EC1Y 8QE

Printed in the United States of America

**Library of Congress Cataloging in Publication Data**

Miller, Gerald R
   Videotape on trial.
   (People and communication; v. 7)
   Bibliography: p.
   1. Video tapes in courtroom proceedings—United States.
I. Fontes, Norman E., joint author.
II. Title.

KF8725.M54   347'.73'75   79-18774
ISBN 0-8039-0967-5
ISBN 0-8039-0968-3 pbk.

FIRST PRINTING

# CONTENTS

# ACKNOWLEDGMENTS

The success of an applied research program such as the one which is the topic of this text hinges on the assistance and cooperation of many persons. This research assessing the use of videotape in the trial process has taken over four years to complete and we owe a debt of gratitude to many individuals who have provided us with both encouragement and assistance. For helping us obtain court facilities and jurors, for playing himself in several of our reenacted trials, and for serving on our Research Advisory Panels, we would particularly like to thank Judge Dale A. Riker of the 68th District Court, Flint, Michigan. From inception to completion, no other person has been more consistently supportive of the research than this dedicated jurist.

Wc would also like to express our thanks to others who have served on our Research Advisory Panels including: Dean Thomas Brennan, Cooley Law School; Mr Joseph Ebersole, Deputy Director of the Federal Judicial Center; Dr Frederick Huszagh, Executive Director, Dean Rusk Center for International and Comparative Law, University of Georgia; Judge James McCrystal, Sandusky, Ohio; Mr Allan Morrill, Attorney; Mr Thomas Murray, Jr., Attorney; Mr Eugene Sattler, C.S.R.; Mr Steven Shiffrin, Attorney; Mr Douglas Swcct, Attorney; and Mr Edward Stein, Attorney.

Other jurists and court administrators have also rendered valuable assistance: Judge James Giddings, Lansing, Michigan; Judge Albert P. Horrigan, Flint, Michigan; Judge Daniel E. Tschirhart, East Lansing, Michigan; and Judge Thomas Yeotis, Genessee County, Michigan. Court administrators such as Arthur Chettle, Flint, Michigan; Albert Kirschenbauer and Gordon Grinwis, Lansing, Michigan; Howard Hanchett, Corunna, Michigan; and Bailiff Lofton Carlton, Genessee County, Michigan aided us in scheduling times for the research and involving jurors. We would also like to thank Mr Steven Brown, Attorney, Kalamazoo, Michigan, for the valuable assistance he rendered during our research.

In addition to these individuals, we would like to thank the expert directors of our reenacted trials, Mr Gerry Dahlmann and Dr Donald Marine, and the excellent casts they assembled. We very much appreciated the assistance of Francis Limmex, Douglas Trusell, John Barrie, and Lynn Beavis for contributing to the design and conduct of the research in a variety of ways.

Over the course of four years, numerous individuals from the Department of Communication have served on our research teams. We sincerely appreciate the substantial contributions they have made to this research. We would like to thank specific individuals for the contributions they have made to various chapters of the text: Ms Joyce Bauchner, Chapter 7; Mr David C. Bender, Chapters 3 and 5; Dr F. Joseph Boster, Chapters 3 and 4; Dr David Brandt, Chapter 7; Mr Robert Bundens, Chapters 5 and 6; Professor Gordon Dahnke, Chapter 6; Mr Thomas Florence, Chapter 3; Ms Lynn Fraedrich, Chapter 5; Dr John Hocking, Chapter 7; Dr Edmund Kaminski, Chapters 5 and 7; Dr Henry Nicholson, Chapter 3; Ms Jennifer Shelby, Chapter 5; and Dr Michael Sunnafrank, Chapters 2 and 5. Most of these individuals have left Michigan State University to assume professional roles elsewhere. Not only do we miss the intellectual stimulation they provided, but we also miss their keen senses of humor which added to the enjoyment of doing this research.

Some of the research discussed in this text was completed with financial support of the National Science Foundation Grants No. GI 38398 and APR75-15815. We are extremely grateful for this support. However, the opinions, findings, conclusions, and recommendations expressed herein are ours and do not necessarily reflect the views of the foundation.

Finally, we would like to thank Dr Arthur Konopka of the National Science Foundation who provided useful criticism and guidance. He was consistently supportive and fulfilled a valuable liaison role between our research team and members of the legal and social scientific communities which facilitated an exchange of ideas that undoubtedly enhanced the quality of our research.

# FOREWORD

The legal system in the United States is overtaxed. As the complexity of our society continues to increase, so do the number of laws intended to maintain social order. A growing number of infractions of these laws, due in part to a difficult economic situation, has increased the number of cases litigated in our court systems. The courts have been unable to process this expanding caseload, and serious backlogs have developed. In some jurisdictions, these backlogs have dramatically increased the time involved in litigation, rendering the promise of justice just that—a promise.

Information-processing problems are not limited to the legal system. We are experiencing a tremendous information explosion in most segments of society. The vast amount of information that must be handled by business enterprises, educational institutions, and government agencies has stimulated a growing interest in audiovisual media, including video technology, as tools for information management. Members of the legal community have contributed to this growing interest by seeking more efficient and more effective ways of processing information.

The possible uses of video technology in the legal system are varied; indeed, with the continuing acceleration of technology, the scope of human imagination defines the outer limits of speculation. As former Attorney General Ramsey Clark observed at a meeting organized by the authors several years ago in New Orleans, "Mass media technology; including Telstar satellites, videotape casettes, and cable television; enables us to bring any knowledge, to any place, in any language, at any time." Because of this wide-ranging potential; jurists, lawyers, and other members of the legal system have scrutinized video technology closely. Their careful scrutiny has stimulated considerable controversy. Proponents of wider use of such media as videotape argue that it will reduce the amount of time involved in litigation, increase the fairness of trials by editing out inadmissable testimony, and allow more efficient use of jurors' time. Opponents of videotape variously view it as à gimmick, a devious way to replace court reporters, and an ominous portent of an electronic legal circus.

It was in this climate that we initiated our program of research designed to assess the effects of videotape trial presentations upon juror information processing and decision-making. Our interest in this area sprang from a desire to investigate systematically a significant communication problem which limits the case-processing effectiveness of courts. We have never believed that employing video technology will *solve* this problem. Nevertheless, we assumed that the severity of information management problems confronting the courts could be *reduced* if videotape presentations could be used to augment live presentations. Adoption of this innovation required a clear demonstration that videotape trial presentations do not produce jury decisions significantly different from those rendered during totally live trials. The research presented in this volume addressed this issue.

Our overall findings reveal no reason that would preclude the use of videotape in the courtroom, although specific findings do indicate a need for policy governing the type of video-recording medium used (monochromatic or color), the type of editing techniques employed to delete testimony and evidence ruled inadmissible, and the type of camera shots used to record testimony provided by different kinds of witnesses. Even though differences in juror information processing stemming from these dimensions of video technology were observed, the verdicts and final awards of jurors during videotape trial presentations did not differ significantly from those of jurors viewing live presentations.

We have attempted to discuss our research in a manner comprehensible to individuals who have little familiarity with social science research techniques. The book will be of interest to those concerned with pursuing additional research in this area as well as members of the legal community such as judges, attorneys, court reporters, and court administrators.

We owe a debt of gratitude to members of the legal community who demonstrated a continuing interest in our research. This cooperative spirit is indicative of the changing times in which we live. A decade ago, behavioral research of this kind would not have received a fair hearing let alone constructive support. As one of the authors recently observed in a chapter published in a volume titled *Psychology and the Legal Process:*

> Legal professionals and social scientists have only recently begun a persistent, if somewhat hesitant, intellectual courtship. To be sure, history has witnessed occasional attempts by one suitor to woo the affections of the other, but these infrequent advances have resembled shotgun weddings more closely than mutually compatible professional marriages. Events of the last few decades, however, have strengthened the vows of both parties, and future annulment or divorce grows increasingly unlikely.

This book was prepared keeping this cooperative spirit in mind. The verdict is not in on videotape, but it is time to deliberate. We have shut down our cameras, turned off the lights, and submitted our evidence for the reader's judgment.

*—G. R. M.*

*1*

# EXAMINING THE SOCIAL AND LEGAL CONTEXT

One zealous advocate of wider use of prerecorded videotaped trials, Judge James McCrystal of the Erie County Court of Common Pleas, Sandusky, Ohio, is fond of remarking that most members of the legal profession are 100% in favor of progress and 1000% opposed to change. Though Judge McCrystal utters it with critical intent, this assertion can be taken nonpejoratively as exemplifying the basic conservatism of our legal institutions. With its roots firmly planted in a venerable tradition of English common law, the legal system of our country is not given to capricious tinkering with basic assumptions and procedures that have withstood the test of time. Chief Justice Warren Burger has observed that "Since lawyers and judges are accustomed to certain habits of procedure, and the very nature of the common-law system depends upon precedent to a large extent, we tend to be wedded to precedent and there is bound to be resistance to change" (1977: 22). Moreover, we suspect that most thoughtful citizens would agree with the system's conservative bent: though social and political institutions are almost certain to atrophy if viewed as entirely sacrosanct, a casual "change for change's sake" attitude is likely to breed the cynicism and disrespect for basic social processes which so concerned that giant of British conservative thought, Edmund Burke.

The preceding paragraph seeks to establish a broad frame of reference for this book, which reports the findings of a series of studies dealing with juror responses to videotaped trial materials. Obviously, the use of taped depositions and trials represents a radical departure from accepted courtroom procedure — as for that matter, does the presentation of expert witnesses' testimony by video telephone in Maricopa County, Arizona (Eliot et al., 1976) and the conduct of welfare hearings by telephone in the state of New Mexico (Corsi, 1978). Nor are such departures, made possible by the burgeoning array of available communication technology, limited to courtroom trials. The potential exists for the new technology to invade every nook and cranny of the legal system. Maricopa County has experimented with numerous applications of the video telephone including in-custody arraignments, public defender conferences with jailed clients, calendar calls, presentencing interviews of convicted inmates, and remote access to police information bureaus (Eliot et al., 1976). The trusty court reporter trumpets the possible benefits of computer-assisted transcription. Indeed, experimental facilities such as McGeorge School of Law's "Courtroom of the Future" are designed with an eye toward maximizing the effectiveness of available communication technology; for instance, a table for displaying exhibits to jurors is positioned under a television camera in the ceiling, thereby permitting a closeup of the exhibit.

To what extent should the legal system hasten to embrace these communication innovations? The answer to this question depends on a number of complex social, economic, and political considerations. We do not attempt an answer in this book, nor do we argue for a particular resolution of the issue. As we have already suggested, changes in our legal institutions must be approached cautiously, lest policy-makers be guilty of throwing out the judicial baby with the bath water. Still, the courts are presently faced with numerous perplexing problems, several of which will be discussed later in this chapter. If judicious use of communication technology can aid in solving these problems, *while at the same time avoiding creation of more thorny difficulties*, changes in traditional courtroom procedures may be justified. The modest goal of the research reported here was to investigate one potential pitfall of using videotaped court materials: the possibility that juror information-processing and decision-making behaviors might be negatively influenced by watching taped trials and depositions. If such negative influences were to occur, they would pose a strong argument against extensive use of videotape in trial settings; conversely, if no negative effects were observed, the case for courtroom use of videotape would be strengthened. By itself, however, neither set of findings would constitute a sovereign indictment or endorsement of taped testimony and trials; rather, the evidence gained would have to be assimilated into a more comprehensive position regarding the social, economic, and political assets or liabilities of such changes in trial procedures.

## TWO CHARACTERISTICS OF TRIALS AS COMMUNICATION EVENTS

Among the many ways it can be described and conceptualized, a view of the trial as a communication event is central to our research interest. When viewed in this way, at least two characteristics are particularly important: first, trials typically occur in face-to-face settings with no mechanical, mediated communication linkages; second, both the structure and content of exchanged courtroom messages are highly rule-governed so as to conform to numerous assumptions regarding the fairest, most just procedures for conducting hearings. Though some of these assumptions have been supported by the research of behavioral scientists, their origins rest in the commonsense, intuitive experiences of jurists and other legal experts. This fact itself poses an intriguing dilemma when expert belief and empirical outcomes differ, a situation which has occurred on more than one occasion.

That trials have traditionally been presented "live" rather than on film or tape is not surprising, since both media are relative Johnny-come-latelys on the communication scene. Moreover, by carefully designing the architectural, sartorial, and other nonverbal trappings of this face-to-face confrontation, considerable credibility was conferred on the judicial system itself; the symbolism which culminates in the "majesty of the courtroom' and in the status and esteem accorded "his honor, the judge" did not develop haphazardly, but was carefully planned and cultivated so as to confer legitimacy on the courts as an instrument for the peaceful resolution of disputes. "Legal and political procedures, such as trials and elections," says Kenneth Boulding, "are essentially social rituals designed to minimize the cost of conflict" (1975: 423). His remark captures one of the objectives that many persons ascribe to a trial, and its realization requires that most members of the society perceive the courts positively.

Aside from the ritualistic impact of the live setting, conventional wisdom also holds that truth is more likely to out — or at worst, credibility and demeanor are likely to receive their sternest tests — when legal adversaries are eyeball-to-eyeball in the courtroom. To interpose a medium such as videotape is to erect a barrier before the jurors' eyes and to provide a psychic haven for the unscrupulous attorney, litigant, or witness. Of course, this judgment is not shared by all members of the legal system, but it is unquestionably the majority viewpoint. Whether there is strong empirical evidence to support this conventional wisdom is a matter commented on in subsequent chapters.

Finally, the presumption lies strongly with the live trial simply becuase it provides the existing standard for comparison. As we remarked several years ago at a conference on the legal and ethical implications of taped trials held at Kent State University (Moore and Landis, 1975), if trials had been conducted on videotape for the past several hundred years, a proposal to commence holding them live would stimulate many of the same questions and objections that have been raised by skeptics and opponents of wider adoption of tape in the courtroom. Consider, for instance, the implications of a question we have encountered on several occasions: might it not be the case that some witnesses will appear less (or more) attractive on videotape than they appear live? Or to mention another frequently encountered query: might not some attorneys be less (or more) persuasive on videotape than in a live setting? Clearly, the answers to these questions, as well as others like them, are affirmative. But what is proved by such answers? If some witnesses look less attractive on tape than in face-to-face settings, the implication is that the persuasive impact of their testimony in a taped trial may be reduced, thus penalizing the litigant who their testimony supports. Nevertheless, the same reasoning holds true for a live trial; i.e., if a witness looks less attractive live than on tape, the persuasive impact of his or her testimony in a live trial will be reduced. Even so, the potential inequity of this latter situation is typically overlooked or ignored since it has existed for centuries. In other words, possible shortcomings of live trials are taken as givens, but when a new medium for transmitting trial information is made available, the same possible shortcomings become fair game for criticism. This discrepancy illustrates one way that the inertia of custom and tradition operates in favor of the status quo, not only in the court system but in most aspects of society.

Besides being carried on in a face-to-face setting, courtroom communication is rigidly rule-governed. Even though most battle-scarred jurists and attorneys realize it is an idealized conception, the image of a trial as a rational, rule-governed event whose mission is the search for truth pervades our society. Miller and Boster have explained the popularity of this image thusly:

> The concept of *dialectic* represents a common thread in a 2,400 year-old tapestry of Western philosophy... Underlying this faith

in dialectic is the commonsense assumption that objective events actually occur and that what is necessary is a method for ascertaining what "really exists" or what "really happened." Dialectic supposedly provides this method through the vehicle of rational, rule-governed argument among reasonable persons who are capable of both knowing and reporting what *is* the case. In a sense, dialectic guides those engaged in it along the path of *episteme* in much the same way that several persons assemble the pieces of a puzzle [1977: 23].

To be sure, the actual conduct of trials departs from the traditional view of dialectic. While Plato and Aristotle conceived of the process as a disinterested search for truth, the adversarial nature of our court system ensures that the trained dialecticians (the attorneys) representing the contesting parties will not perceive their task in the same way. Attorneys can more aptly be characterized as carrying on a process of *interested dialectic*: rather than sifting alternative arguments and evidence to assemble a case most closely approximating "truth", they peruse information selectively so as to arrive at the most persuasive case for their clients. Because of the strong ego involvement associated with "winning" the case, rules impose important communication constraints and obligations on the actions of the contesting parties.

More specifically, those rules guiding the conduct of trials reflect the efforts of distinguished jurists and other legal scholars to "legislate" patterns of behavior that coincide with accepted philosophical premises concerning the nature of fair, just legal hearings. For instance, the concept of *presumption* holds that defendants are to be presumed innocent and that the burden of proof therefore lies with the prosecution. Consequently, if there are any advantages for either party inextricably bound up in trial procedures, they should favor the defendant. One inherent feature of a trial is that one of the contesting parties must have the last word. If this last word is advantageous, the concept of presumption mandates that it should be uttered by the defendant's attorney. Conversely, if the chance to present closing arguments first confers a persuasive edge, the defense and prosecution speaking order should be reversed. It was an interest in this specific question that stimulated the early research on primacy and recency (Lund, 1925): whether, ceteris paribus, inherent persuasive advantage results from presenting an argument first (primacy) or last (recency). To admit that some fifty years and scores of studies have not produced a definitive answer to the question (McGuire, 1969) in no way negates its importance, nor does it suggest that jurists should cease periodic stocktaking of trial procedures in order to determine if changes are warranted by the empirical state-of-the-art.

No doubt the reader can think of many similar examples of how judicial rules reflect attempts to bring trial conduct into line with prevailing norms of justice. Of particular interest here, however, are those situations where the face-to-face context of the trial may conflict with ensuring the effectiveness of the rules. Two examples illustrate our concern. Everyone is familiar with the dramatic cliché centering on the introduction of a particularly damaging question or comment by an attorney, a heated objection by the opposing lawyer, and the judge's concluding injunction, "The objection is sustained and the jury is instructed to disregard the last remark." There are strong grounds for questioning whether the judge's verbal imposition of a rule can completely overcome the psychological reality of the illicit information on jury members. To the extent that these grounds are justified, conducting the trial in a face-to-face setting prevents stringent enforcement of the rules of admissibility, since rule-violating material cannot be expunged before it intrudes on the jury's psyche. Conversely, the use of some mediated system, such as film or videotape, allows court officials to edit inadmissible testimony before the jury hears the case. We will say more about this potential advantage of videotape later.

Even when inadmissible material is not deliberately introduced, realization of particular legal values may be impossible in a live setting. The mere act of observing some features of a litigant may be sufficient to bias jurors for or against the litigant's case. Prior research shows that a defendant's physical attractiveness influences the severity of recommended punishment (Dion, 1972; Efran, 1974), though the relationship is complex and influenced by such factors as whether the crime itself is attractiveness-related (Sigall and Ostrove, 1975). Similarly, an individual's ethnic or racial affiliation may result in juror prejudice, particularly if there are obvious cues pointing to the affiliation. In many jurisdictions, Blacks may be unable to secure an unbiased day in court. At a workshop held in New Orleans several years ago, former Attorney General Ramsey Clark emphasized this possibility by pointing out that of the thousands convicted of rape since 1931, only 455 were sentenced to death, and of the number, 405 were Black. Notwithstanding the traditional guarantee of the right of confrontation in criminal cases, defendants of certain ethnic and racial origins might receive fairer treatment if the jury remained ignorant of race or ethnic identity. Indeed, the right of confrontation could conceivably be satisfied by allowing the defendant to view the proceedings on television in surroundings removed from the courtroom proper. The facility at the McGeorge School of Law, mentioned earlier, includes a room adjacent to the court where defendants may be placed to view the trial, the intent of such an arrangement being to avoid Chicago Seven-type incidents by promptly removing unruly defendants from the courtroom. What we have suggested implies that it might be desirable to keep all defendants out of the court so their physical, racial, or ethnic characteristics do not bias the outcomes of their cases.

We have outlined a view of the trial as a communication event to provide a perspective regarding more extensive adoption of videotaped trials and depositions. Use of the tape medium violates the traditional concept that trials should occur in face-to-face settings. Because of this presumption favoring the live trial, those who advocate wider use of videotape must demonstrate convincingly that it will not exert a deleterious influence on the trial process. Conversely, videotape provides the opportunity, at least in principle, to eliminate some troublesome aspects of contemporary courtroom procedures. For instance, we have noted that inadmissible material could be removed without the jury ever being aware of it, a procedure more closely conforming with the judicial values underlying the rules of admissibility. In short, when we consider the present conception of the trial as a communication event, the appearance of videotape on the scene has both pluses and minuses associated with it.

## THE POSSIBLE ROLE OF VIDEOTAPE IN DEALING WITH CONTEMPORARY COURTROOM PROBLEMS

It is estimated that more than ten million civil petitions are filed annually in state courts alone. Addressing the monumental logjams occurring in our courts today, Chief Justice Burger has asserted that "we in America make excessive use of our courts. It's often been said — and I think it's probably true — that the American people are the most litigous people in the world...Many seem to think that we should settle all of our disputes in the courts" (1977: 21). Given the American citizen's tendency to look to the courts for solutions whenever conflicts arise, it is hardly surprising that the dockets in most jurisdictions are overloaded and that people must often wait for several years for their cases to come to trial.

Many legal experts have argued that sheer case volume is not the only reason why justice often moves at a procedural snail's pace. The procedures embodied in the live trial also exact a toll in time and energy. Considerable time is consumed by objections, bench conferences, delays for witnesses, counsel's pauses, client conferences, and chamber retreats. Sometimes, a case may drag on for several days or weeks only to be settled by the contestants without bringing the trial to conclusion. Because of these occurrences, jurors feel their time is not spent wisely; for many, a typical term of jury service entails precious few hours of hearing cases in the courtroom but many days of marking time in the jury room. Ironically, a story several years ago in the Lansing *State Journal* (1975), which described jurors' dissatisfaction with jury service, concluded by noting one juror's lament that time would go faster if a television set were installed in the jury room.

Advocates of more extensive use of videotaped trial materials contend that this medium has the potential to increase dramatically the number of cases that can be heard. Praising the added efficiency of prerecorded videotaped trials, Judge Mc-Crystal describes his experiences in eliminating a backlog of highway and urban renewal appropriations cases in Trumbull County, Ohio:

> Aware of the apparent success of the prerecorded trial procedure in Erie County, Chief Justice O'Neill of the Ohio Supreme Court in the fall of 1975 assigned me to some 180 highway and urban renewal appropriations cases then pending in Trumbull County, with instructions to use prerecorded trials. A majority of these cases had been pending from three to six years. Trumbull County, the tenth largest county in Ohio, was literally innundated with appropriations cases. The three resident judges were unable to keep their dockets current.
>
> In 1976 more than a hundred appropriation cases were ordered prerecorded. Of these, fifty-three were terminated by prerecorded jury trial, and the balance were settled. The highest number of appropriation cases terminated by jury trial in Trumbull County before 1976 was twenty-five. I edited more than sixty of these trials and presided over twenty-five in seventeen trial days, using two courtrooms. The resident judges presided over the remaining edited trials. This added innovation raised no problems [McCrystal, 1977: 978-979].

How does videotaping produce such a dramatic increase in the number of cases tried? To answer this question, a brief explanation of the taped trial's preparation and presentation is necessary. The contesting attorneys prepare taped depositions of all the witnesses in the trial. At the time each deposition is taken, the attorneys lodge any objections they wish to raise, and using the digital counter of the recorder, log the points on the tape where the objections occur. Working in chambers, the presiding judge listens to the relevant testimony and rules on the objections. If an objection is sustained, the material is edited from the ongoing trial; if it is overruled, the material is presented to the jury. The end product is a package of taped depositions containing all the trial testimony with the inadmissible material identified so jurors will not be privy to it.

At the appointed time, the jury is assembled to hear the trial. Typically, the attorneys present their opening remarks live. Testimony of witnesses for the plaintiff and defense then proceeds as scheduled on tape. A bailiff or other court official operates the recorder, and jurors watch the testimony on several strategically placed monitors. As described more fully in Chapter 5, several techniques are available for editing inadmissible material from the trial. The most frequently used procedure requires the person operating the recorder to suppress both the audio and visual channels and either to allow the machine to run at normal speed, if the objectionable material is relatively brief; or to fast-forward the tape, if the material consumes considerable time. In opening remarks to the jury, the judge informs them that inadmissible testimony will be deleted in this way so that the jurors understand why the audio and visual have been suppressed. This method of editing eliminates the need to cut and splice the tape, a definite plus in this post-Watergate era when suspicions of tampering and subversion are relatively commonplace.

After hearing all taped testimony, the jurors listen to the closing arguments of the attorneys, receive their instructions from the judge, and retire to deliberate. Since the judge has previously ruled on all objections, he or she need not be in court while testimony is being played for the jury. Instead, the judge can spend the time in chambers listening to other taped depositions and ruling on attorneys' objections. While some legal experts believe the credibility of the trial is compromised by a judge's absence, proponents of videotape such as Judge McCrystal contend that their time is used more wisely preparing future trials rather than sitting idly on the bench while witnesses testify.

Jurors hear a version of the trial uninterrupted by bench conferences, chamber retreats, and recessed time. Once such interruptions have been eliminated, the average "running time" for most trials is surprisingly short. This fact explains the large number of cases Judge McCrystal was able to dispose of in a relatively brief time. Furthermore, it provides at least a partial explanation why over 75% of the videotaped trial jurors interviewed by researchers from the Law and Justice Center of Battelle Institute (Bermant et al., 1975) said they would prefer to have a case in which they were involved presented on tape rather than in a live setting: they indicated that the continuous flow of information reduced distraction, enhanced concentration, and permitted more effective use of their time.

The phrase "more effective use of time" is central to most arguments used to support wider use of prerecorded videotaped trials. No one contends that judges, attorneys, or jurors will have to spend less time or work less diligently if videotaped trials become more commonplace. Rather, people who support taped trial materials argue that these groups will be able to use their time and energy more wisely. Whether or not this is true, it seems clear that taping trials would result in greater efficiency insofar as the total number of trials that could be processed and heard by juries.

Even when a live trial is progressing with dispatch, the absence of a single witness can result in considerable delay. Videotaped depositions can combat this problem, for they permit attorneys to prerecord the testimony of a witness and to insert it at the appropriate spot in the trial. Consider, for instance, the plight of expert witnesses: psychiatrists, engineers, economists, or other persons whose knowledge of a certain area causes them to be called frequently to testify. Obviously, the schedules of these individuals do not allow them to sit around the court for days waiting to be called. Sometimes when the attorney is ready for their testimony, they are not in court and the trial must be recessed until they arrive. This results in Hobson's choice: either these expert witnesses can be inconvenienced by requiring their presence until they offer testimony, or the trial can be delayed while they are summoned to court.

By videotaping the testimony of expert witnesses, this dilemma can be resolved. The procedure used is exactly the same as for the entire prerecorded videotaped trial. The deposition is taken with both attorneys present, and during testimony, they lodge and log their objections. The presiding judge listens to the objectionable material and rules on it. The taped deposition is then set aside and played at the elected time, with the court official in charge of the monitor editing the inadmissible material.

Videotaping can also be used to take testimony of geographically distant witnesses, reducing the cost and time involved in securing their testimony. During an Air Force court-martial held in Korea several years ago, testimony of several witnesses stationed in the United States was taped and flown to Korea, thus eliminating the cost of transporting witnesses to the Far East. Former President Ford's taped testimony in the trial of Lynette Fromm combines elements of both the preceding situations: not only did his busy schedule make it difficult for him to take the necessary time to offer live testimony, the cost of transporting him back and forth across the country would have been much greater than the expense of presenting his testimony via tape.

A third possible application of videotaped depositions lies in taking testimony of witnesses who find it difficult or impossible to be in court at the time of trial. This application sometimes poses difficult issues of admissibility. For example, were it virtually certain that a terminally ill witness would not survive long enough to testify at the trial, the testimony could be videotaped. Assuming the opposing attorney had the chance to cross-examine when the deposition was taken, the testimony might be admissible even though the witness had died in the interim. As yet, no firm precedence has been established on this question. An even more troublesome area involves taking depositions from physically incapacitated persons, particularly if their injuries or sickness are directly related to the case. Though the anecdote may be apocryphal, we have heard of an attorney who taped the deposition of an accident plaintiff in the latter's hospital bed with a plethora of traction devices, catheter tubes, and plasma bottles plainly visible. Allegedly, the judge refused to admit the deposition on the grounds that the physical surroundings were excessively biasing.

Proponents of using videotaped depositions argue they are both cost-effective and time-efficient. Unlike the prerecorded videotaped trial, however, a single taped deposition psychologically intrudes on an otherwise live milieu. This intrusion raises the question of whether jurors might respond differently to the testimony of the taped witness than to the rest of the trial. The fact that the testimony has been committed to tape may confer it a disproportionate persuasive advantage, particularly if jurors interpret the deviation as arising from the added importance of the witness. On the other hand, appearing on tape could excessively blunt the testimony's impact, especially if the witness were not very effective on the medium. These possibilities are examined more fully in Chapter 3.

Not only are courts of original jurisdiction crowded, appellate schedules are also expanding rapidly. Chief Justice Burger (1977) cites a 20-year increase from 3,700 to 19,000 in the number of cases appearing before United States courts of appeal. Similarly, the Supreme Court's docket has grown from 2,000 to 4,700 cases in the past 20 years. Advocates of videotape contend its expanded use for trials and depositions can sharply reduce the number of judicial decisions leading to appeal. In the live courtroom, judges must often rule quickly on motions and objections, thus enhancing the likelihood of error. When individual depositions or trials are precorded, issues of law can be pondered at relative leisure in chambers. This added time for thought and research could reasonably be expected to reduce the number of reversible decisions.

There is, however, another side to this coin. Traditionally, appeals based on inappropriate nonverbal demeanor by judges or other court officials have been impossible since no record of these behaviors existed. Videotape captures many of these nonverbal activities. Consequently, if videotape were to be used instead of, or in addition to, a typed transcript to preserve the trial record (yet a third possible use not directly addressed in the research we will report), issues concerning facial or bodily decorum would be at least potentially appealable. Whether the appellate courts would agree to hear these types of appeals remains uncertain, although the consensus among legal experts with whom we have visited is that courts of appeal would be reluctant to admit them. Still, to point to a relatively recent example, had the trials of the Watergate defendants been recorded on videotape, questions raised by Judge Sirica's nonverbal actions could conceivably have become grounds for appeal. If a precedent were established for hearing such appeals, the gains achieved through reduction of other errors could be largely offset.

Finally, such supporters of videotape as Judge McCrystal, the late Ohio Supreme Court Chief Justice O'Neill, and attorney Thomas Murray Jr. contend that wider use of taped depositions will reduce attorney histrionics and eliminate the circus-like atmosphere that sometimes develops in trials. Without the presence of a jury, attorneys would be less likely to showboat when questioning witnesses, and the trial would focus more closely on the relative merits of opposing arguments and evidence. Although the overall extent to which questionable courtroom tactics would be curbed by videotaping is impossible to assess, the argument's merits must be granted in at least one area. Judges and attorneys agree that many lawyers now bring up matters they know will be ruled inadmissible on the assumption that, having heard the material, the jury will be favorably influenced by it. If depositions were taped, the motivation to employ this tactic would no longer exist since the inadmissible material would be edited before jurors saw the tape.

Again, skeptics of the merits of videotaping counter with a scenario that envisions not only an increase in courtroom drama, but also one that will be particularly beneficial to economically advantaged litigants. These skeptics suspect that wealthy clients will hire skilled television directors to assist attorneys in recording depositions. Through expert use of such techniques as panning, zooming, and switching; the testimony of witnesses could be presented in a maximally favorable light. To carry the argument to its logical extreme, cases might eventually be decided on the basis of which litigant was able to engage the best director of testimony.

There are at least two reasons why such extreme eventualities are unlikely. First, as more jurisdictions adopt videotape, they will probably develop uniform legal rules for its use. Already several states have promulgated such rules, and typically, they restrict the alternatives available to camera operators to a limited number of simple, straightforward shots. Second, elaborate effects require elaborate equipment, and while extremely wealthy clients might be able to access such facilities, the typical attorney's taping studio contains a limited amount of hardware. Consequently, the depositions used in trials usually consist of a fixed shot of the head and upper body of the witness, and in some instances, the attorneys. Hence, neither the legal nor economic realities of the situation are likely to permit production of testimonial extravaganzas. We do, however, report the results of several studies dealing with simple production techniques in Chapter 6.

Thus far, we have mentioned two courtroom uses of videotape (prerecorded videotaped trials and individual depositions) which are dealt with in the research described here and one which is not (videotaping the trial for record). In the spirit of exhaustiveness, we want to mention a fourth use, taping demonstrative evidence. Rather than taking jurors to the scene of an event, videotape makes it possible to record the scene and bring it to the courtroom. Moreover, the flexibility provided by porta-packs and hand-held cameras permits taping of numerous ingenious demonstrations, many of which are subject to questions of admissibility.

One example should be sufficient to illustrate. In southern

Ohio some years ago, two friends were returning from an evening of imbibing, each driving his own car. As the driver of the lead car attempted to turn into his driveway, he missed the road and entered the ditch. His friend parked his car behind the car in the ditch and across the highway. While the two men were attempting to connect the cars with a chain, another motorist smashed into the car on the road, killing one of the men. The motorist was subsequently tried for negligent homicide.

The major issue of the trial was whether the motorist could have been expected to stop in the time he had after seeing the car across the road. Since it was agreed by all parties that his car was traveling about fifty miles an hour, the defense arranged for a car to be placed across the road in the same spot; for a driver to drive down the road at fifty miles an hour; and for a cameraman, standing on the floor behind the front seat, to shoot tape through the front windshield to obtain a perspective on how much stopping distance remained when the car came into view. Since there was disagreement as to whether the parked car's lights were lit, the demonstration was taped twice, once with the lights on and once with them off.

Although the prosecution objected, the judge allowed the videotapes to be shown. The result was a hung jury, and the defendant was released from custody. Clearly, videotape has almost unlimited potential as a tool for producing demonstrative evidence, and when employed as in the preceding example, admissibility is almost certain to be tested on each occasion.

## SUMMING UP

This chapter has sketched a social and legal context for reporting our research on jurors' responses to videotaped trial materials. We have described two important characteristics of the trial when viewed as a communication event, concluding with the observation that, as far as these characteristics are concerned, videotape has both pluses and minuses associated with it. We have also outlined some of the major problems faced by today's courts and have summarized several of the arguments concerning ways that videotaped trial materials can solve or alleviate these problems.

In the chapters that follow, we examine whether or not jurors respond differently to videotaped than to live trials and testimony. To anticipate and deal with a number of questions that may be raised, our next chapter describes and justifies the procedural assumptions which guided our program of inquiry; particularly those relating to the reenactment, or simulation, of trials and depositions.

*2*

# METHODOLOGICAL ISSUES

Several arguments have been leveled against social science research dealing with the trial and jury processes in general, and against our own research on videotaped trial materials in particular. Our analysis of and response to these criticisms seek to provide a framework for evaluating the research findings to be discussed in subsequent chapters, primarily by explaining our decisions concerning certain crucial substantive and methodological issues.

Most criticisms of our research have been raised during face-to-face conversations. They generally fall into one of three categories: (1) the argument from uniqueness; (2) the argument from complexity; and (3) the argument against simulations and replications. The first two of these arguments can be dealt with quickly, while the third requires a more extensive analysis.

The argument from uniqueness embraces a general proposition that has been used to indict any scientific study of human behavior, not just research dealing with communication in the legal system. Simply stated, advocates of this position argue that all individuals are unique, as are the interactions among them. Consequently, knowledge gained by observing a given interaction cannot be generalized to other interactions.

Despite the intuitive appeal of this argument, it poses no formidable barrier to our research. While it is true that many behaviors are unique to specific individuals, it is equally true that many other behaviors are shared among individuals. Such behavioral sharing facilitates development and maintenance of an organized society. Regularity in human behavior permits researchers to employ scientific methods capable of discovering these regularities. Unquestionably, all the variability in human behavior cannot be accounted for, but research can be profitable in those situations where there is reason to believe behavioral regularities exist. The argument from uniqueness would only invalidate our research if there were no regularities in human behavior within a trial or among trial participants across trials.

The second objection to legal communication research, the argument from complexity, relies on the premise that there are so many variables operating in the courtroom environment that it is impossible to produce useful empirical generalizations about the trial process. Certainly this argument is not without merit. Indeed, a trial may be a relatively complex phenomenon, and it may be difficult to discover parsimonious explanatory statements that increase understanding of the trial process. Implicitly, however, this argument assumes that the legal system is more complex than other aspects of human behavior for which useful generalizations have been developed. When we consider the complexities inherent in interpersonal, organizational, and mass communication — to name a few areas in which empirical generalizations have been developed — it seems unlikely that the legal system is somehow more complex and difficult to study.

## ARGUMENTS AGAINST SIMULATIONS AND REPLICATIONS

The argument against simulations and replications is the third objection voiced by skeptics of our research. This objection is somewhat elusive because of the numerous meanings assigned to the words "simulation" and "replication" by individuals who use them. Bermant et al. (1974) tried to develop a semantic perspective that would enable them to specify useful conceptual definitions for these terms when evaluating social science research focusing upon the legal system. This chore was a formidable one since several complex philosophical arguments for and against scientific approaches to the study of human behavior are related to the issue of simulations and replications. Bermant et al. elected not to become embroiled in these philosophical issues and accepted as a given the premise that the scientific method of inquiry can be used to generate knowledge concerning human behavior. We have chosen to follow the same course of action. Readers interested in exploring these philosophical issues are encouraged to examine Krimerman (1969).

## Evaluation Criteria for Models

Bermant et al. discuss three different types of models: simulations, formalizations, and replications. Citing Mihram (1972: 7), they develop a conceptual framework which distinguishes among the three types of models. *Simulation* is defined as a "model in which the components do not have the physical characteristics of the object or system modeled, nor are the workings of the model completely specified by analytic mathematics or computing routines" (1974: 225). Drawing upon Mihram's work, Bermant et al. define *replications* as models "that display a significant degree of physical similarity to that being modeled" (Mihram, 1972: 7). *Formalizations*, on the other hand, are not physically similar to the phenomenon being modeled, but are defined by a set of related symbols manipulated "by means of a well formed discipline such as mathematics or logic" (Mihram, 1972: 7).

Bermant and his colleagues contend that these types of models are evaluated in terms of structural or functional verisimilitude. Structural verisimilitude refers to the extent to which a model is physically identical to the phenomenon being modeled, while functional verisimilitude refers to the success or the "useful equivalence of their conduct under specified conditions to the conduct of the object or system being modeled" (Bermant et al., 1974: 226). Given their definitions for distinguishing among the three types of models, Bermant et al. suggest that simulations and formalizations must be evaluated in terms of functional verisimilitude, while replications must be assessed in terms of structural verisimilitude.

As a result of a general critique of social science research focusing upon the legal system, Bermant et al. offer the following two observations: (1) social scientists have not used replications in their research; and (2) the stimulus presentations employed to model the trial process reflect little concern for structural or functional verisimilitude. The authors subsequently conclude that "there is no empirical reason to believe, in regard to the great bulk of research published to date, that it generalizes to the conduct of real juries" (p. 229). We next consider the implications of both these observations as well as the general conclusion concerning the generalizability of legal research. Moreover, the merit of Bermant's criticisms as they apply to our own research are addressed, even though the research presented here postdates the criticisms of Bermant and his colleagues.

Bermant et al.'s conceptual definition of the term "replication", combined with their assertion that experiments in the physical sciences are typically performed on replications (p. 226), supports the conclusion that most legal studies completed, strictly speaking, are not experiments (p. 228). Moreover, the claim that each "real" trial is a unique event (p. 228) suggests that replications are impossible, and hence the use of experiments in legal research is by fiat also impossible. This claim is somewhat confusing because the authors themselves state that replications are evaluated in terms of structural, not functional verisimilitude. If replications were assessed by their functional verisimilitude, their criticism would be more persuasive since the criterion most logically suited for this type of evaluation would be the verdict rendered by an actual jury in an actual trial.

To further complicate matters, the caveat offered by Bermant and his colleagues relevant to their criticism appears to substitute the term "simulation" for "replication":

> The most obvious difficulty [for researchers] is that every real trial happens only once; it is a unique event. There is no way and little point in trying, from the scientific point of view, to simulate a *particular* trial functionally, for that would mean only that the simulated verdict was the same as the real verdict. Clearly, what is desired is to simulate classes of trials, or classes of events within trials, that may present features of social-psychological interest. In the attempt to do that, however, one runs the risk of abstracting out just the particularities which generated the results in the actual trials [pp. 228-229].

This assertion produces a methodological double-bind that largely precludes the use of social-scientific techniques to investigate the legal system. If a researcher employs simulations of cases already tried and relies upon the actual verdict rendered to assess the functional verisimilitude of the simulation, the assumption must be made that the actual verdict in the case is *correct*, a dubious assumption according to Bermant et al. (p. 232). Since formalizations are completely specified simulations, they suffer from the same limitations for legal researchers as simulations. If researchers subscribed to the conceptual framework and evaluative criteria developed by Bermant, empirical studies focusing upon the trial process would be next to impossible.

While it would be erroneous to dismiss Bermant et al.'s comments concerning some of the psycho-legal research critiques, their conclusion that "the great bulk" of legal research completed up to 1974 is not generalizable to real juries appears to be somewhat of an overstatement. Moreover, using physical sciences as a yardstick for determining the type of model necessary to conduct experimental research without explicitly considering *what* constitutes an experiment closes off the possibility of using simulations for experimental research. No logical mandate compels behavioral scientists to mimic their physical scientist counterparts; indeed, it can be argued that slavish imitation might well retard the development of social science given the differences between phenomena studied by physical and social scientists.

Different research problems mandate different empirical strategies whose success must be evaluated in terms of their predictive and explanatory utility, not by asking how scholars working in other disciplines apply the same strategies to problems of interest to them. The constraints imposed by uniformly adopting or rejecting methods from other disciplines can stifle the ability of the researcher to select a strategy appropriate to the problem. Furthermore, such rigidity sometimes generates controversies which have the intellectual merit of the proverbial chicken and egg dispute.

The criteria offered by Bermant's group for evaluating empirical legal research, structural and functional verisimilitude, appear useful. Nevertheless, it strikes us as curious to evaluate simulations and formalizations solely in terms of functional verisimilitude and to assess replications only on the basis of their structural verisimilitude. This approach seems to imply that no trial stimulus can be developed which is both structurally and functionally verisimilous. Perhaps this limitation exists *if* the assumption is made that deterministic rather than stochastic relationships exist among the variables included in the model — i.e., if one assumes that the predictions made by using the model will always be correct rather than correct some substantial percentage of the time. Although deterministic relationships are obviously most desirable, observed stochastic relationships also have utility and should not be ignored.

## Deterministic Versus Stochastic Knowledge Claims

The success of legal communication researchers at developing either deterministic or stochastic generalizations is greatly influenced by the types of research questions or hypotheses pursued. For instance, trying to predict verdict outcomes in actual trials is a different type of pursuit than trying to predict how verdict outcomes might be influenced by the many variables operating in the courtroom. Successful accomplishment of the first goal presupposes considerable knowledge concerning the second. The research criticized by Bermant et al. which attempted to predict verdict outcomes was perhaps premature given the present limited knowledge concerning factors that may significantly influence juror verdicts; e.g., assessment of the credibility of trial participants, judgments of the truthfulness of testimony, amount and type of information retained from trial proceedings, ethnic affiliation of defendants and plaintiffs, perceived physical attractiveness of trial participants, the effects of introducing inadmissible trial material, and information concerning a defendant's previous convictions.

Bermant and his colleagues also pose three other questions that bear upon the issue of generalizability of legal communication research:

(1) How realistic are the setting and circumstances wherein participants are asked to behave as jurors?
(2) How similar are the participants in the research to persons likely to serve on real juries?
(3) How well does the model mimic the behavior of actual juries behaving under conditions of similar input? (p. 227).

These three issues concern social scientists only if it can be demonstrated that differences between courtroom environments and laboratory settings, study participants and actual jurors, and the trial process and research stimuli differentially influence information-processing and decision-making behaviors of actual and/or role-playing jurors. Such a demonstration poses difficult problems since the most obvious criterion available for making this comparison is the verdict rendered in an actual trial as opposed to the one produced by participants in a research study. Unfortunately, as we mentioned earlier, there is no reason to believe that the verdict produced by an actual trial is the *correct* verdict. Stated differently, a given case tried by two different juries could certainly produce two different verdicts. Nevertheless, it is also reasonable to assume that the trial process will usually produce verdicts warranted by the evidence presented. Just as scientists never research facts per se, but instead evaluate the truth or falsity of *statements* about facts, the trial process is also restricted to statements of fact, assessments of the veracity of these statements, and conclusions that are justifiably warranted by statements *believed* to be true (Miller and Boster, 1977).

A jury's verdict is a statement of fact stipulating that the accused was either guilty or innocent of a particular act. Obviously, this statement can be either true (the defendant *did* or *did not* commit the act) or false (the defendant did commit the act *but* the jurors concluded he or she did not, or the defendant did not commit the act *but* the jurors concluded he or she did). Moreover, a verdict rendered by a judge or an opinion offered by an experienced attorney would imply the same alternatives although there might be less error than with jurors. Consequently, using verdicts rendered by judges in actual trials or expert opinions of attorneys will not solve the problem involved in using verdict outcomes as a means of comparing actual trials to trial stimuli used in research studies.

We are not arguing that verdicts constitute an inappropriate research variable; rather, we are suggesting that verdict comparisons should be restricted to a given trial using comparable participants as jurors. To do this will normally require the use of models to represent the trial process or some particular aspect, such as the use of depositions. Although it is unlikely that the normal cognitive processes of jurors undergo some type of radical change in the courtroom, these processes may be systematically influenced by different modes of presenting the trial-related information used in verdict decisions.

### The Dangers of Unrealistic Simulations

Research by Bermant et al. (1974) and Fontes, Miller and

Sunnafrank (1977) has produced systematic differences in verdict outcomes by varying the procedures used to present trial information. Bermant et al. used four conditions in their study. A murder trial transcript provided the basis for the trial stimulus. One group of participants read a four-page written summary of the trial while a second group read a thirty-one-page trial transcript. Yet a third group listened to an audiotaped presentation of the transcript while a fourth group viewed an audiovisual trial reproduction employing slides accompanied by a recorded narration. Analysis of the individual verdicts of study participants demonstrated that verdict decisions were influenced by the type of stimulus employed; specifically, the more closely the stimulus approximated an actual trial, the greater the number of guilty verdicts returned.

The study by Fontes, Sunnafrank and Miller (1977) produced similar results. With assistance from legal experts, a trial transcript of a felony vehicular manslaughter trial was selected. This particular crime was used because there are no apparent sexual, ethnic, or physical attractiveness stereotypes that are likely to influence juror decisions. The hour and thirty-minute trial was reenacted in a courtroom environment and videotaped in color. The second stimulus used in the study consisted of a twenty-minute video synopsis. A fifteen-second break between presentations of witnesses was edited into the tape permitting use of a voice-over technique to provide information concerning the next witness to testify. Information relevant to the intent and motive of the accused was included in this synopsis. The final stimulus was a 1,161 word written synopsis which contained the same testimony included in the video synopsis.

Role-playing jurors were randomly assigned to one of the three different modes of trial presentation. Each group saw or read the materials and then provided verdicts for the trial. The results revealed that the mode of trial presentation did influence juror judgments. Role-playing jurors exposed to the entire videotaped trial and to the video synopsis returned significantly more guilty verdicts than jurors who read the written synopsis.

These results prompted the following cautionary notes:

> This finding has important implications for researchers who are concerned about the extent to which results obtained in research settings can be generalized to the actual milieu of the courtroom. Although the findings of studies conducted in simulated environments which depart markedly from the presentational and informational characteristics of the courtroom may be of some theoretical value, researchers who employ such procedures should be extremely wary about generalizing to actual trials. Indeed, the results of the...study reported here suggest that if generalizability is a primary consideration, studies should be conducted under presentational and informational conditions which closely approximate the actual courtroom trial. Although this conclusion is far from earthshaking, our findings concerning the effects of mode of presentation *per se* on juror response buttress it with empirical support. The road from laboratory to courtroom appears to be more scientifically and socially hazardous than some prior research on juror behavior would have us believe [p. 19].

In the absence of knowing the "correct" verdict for any given trial, this cautious strategy seems best suited for assessing how trial decisions may be influenced by a host of variables including mode of presentation.

The findings of both Bermant et al.'s (1974) and Fontes et al.'s (1977) studies, while producing different significant trends in verdicts rendered, indicate that findings from studies employing trial stimulus presentations which deviate markedly from the actual trial process may have limited generalizability. Nevertheless, these findings do not warrant a general indictment of studies of the trial process which rely upon stimulus presentations other than an actual trial.

Regardless of the general utility of Bermant et al.'s criteria of structural and functional verisimilitude, they do underscore the need to attend carefully to the degree of correspondence between trial stimulus presentations and actual trials. A similar criterion, *ecological validity*, was advocated by Brunswik (1947) as a means of assessing the generalizability of social-scientific research findings, particularly those derived from laboratory studies. The ecological validity of a study is determined by the variables included or excluded in a study as compared to those present in the actual phenomenon being studied. The greater the number of variables excluded from a given study, the greater the potential threat to its ecological validity, and hence, the generalizability of the findings. Our use of this criterion encompasses both the verisimilitude criteria and is necessitated by our rejection of the claim that experimental methods can only be applied to replications.

Experimental research methods do not necessarily presuppose a high degree of correspondence between the stimulus used in a study and the phenomenon being studied. Given the number of potential available designs, it is next to impossible to detail the specific characteristics of a good experimental design. Lindquist (1953) has listed five essential characteristics of any good design:

(1) It will insure that the observed treatment effects are *unbiased* estimates of the true effects.

(2) It will permit a quantitative description of the precision of the observed treatment effects regarded as estimates of the "true" effects.

(3) It will insure that the observed treatment effects will have whatever degree of precision is required by the broader purposes of the experiment.

(4) It will make possible an objective test of a specific hypothesis concerning the true effects; that is, it will permit the computation of the relative frequency with which the observed discrepancy between the observation and hypothesis would be exceeded if the hypothesis were true.

(5) It will be *efficient*; that is, it will satisfy these requirements at the minimum "cost," broadly conceived (p. 6).

Lindquist defines *true effects* as "the effect that would have been obtained in a perfectly controlled experiment, involving all members of the population from which participants included in the study were drawn" (p. 2). The effects observed in any single experiment are only estimates of the true effects. It is worth noting that no assumptions are made regarding the correspondence between the stimulus used in an experiment and the phenomenon being studied.

Experiments in which trial stimulus presentations of low ecological validity are employed will seldom provide valid estimates of the true effects. Most of our experiments relied upon simulations of the trial process. The ecological validity of each simulation was carefully evaluated to ensure maximum generalizability of the findings. Two criteria guided our development of stimuli for these studies: (1) maximum realism and (2) maximum experimental control. To some extent these are conflicting criteria. Maximum realism could be achieved by gathering our data from actual trials. Unfortunately, the potential threat to fair adjudication of cases eliminated this approach as an acceptable strategy. Moreover, there could be no guarantee that the cases selected would proceed in a typical manner, and any major unanticipated deviations would substantially reduce the generalizability of the findings. Finally, the potential for uncontrolled variables to influence the variables of interest would be enhanced by lack of rigorous experimental control.

Awareness of the degree of experimental control built into a study permits better assessment of the extent to which the stimulus presentation deviates from the phenomenon being investigated. Both generalizability and validity of the findings will be affected by the amount of control imposed. Stated differently, too much control may produce findings that are not really generalizable to the phenomenon being studied even though they may be treated as highly probable knowledge claims. Conversely, lack of experimental control may culminate in propositions where the consequences are attributed to the wrong antecedents or "causes."

## Minimizing Threats to Ecological Validity

With these concerns in mind, we decided to reenact trials in the presence of actual jurors whenever possible. This approach permitted us to achieve a high degree of realism while also maintaining considerable experimental control over extraneous factors that could contaminate research findings. These reenactments constituted simulations of the trial process, not replications. Transcripts of actual trials were used for the reenactments, and we attempted to select actors and actresses with personal characteristics similar to the original trial participants. Actual judges presided during the trial reenactments which were carried out in real courtrooms.

Most of our studies departed from actual trial procedures in two ways. Since they were designed to evaluate the potential effects of videotaped presentations upon juror information processing and decision-making, it was necessary to determine if the alternative presentational modes affected individual juror predeliberation decisions, as well as subsequent deliberation proceedings. Consequently, the jurors participating in most of the studies did not actually deliberate although they were led to beieve they were participating in an actual trial, that they would deliberate, and that the verdict rendered would be binding upon the litigants. Had these jurors been allowed to deliberate, individual juror judgments might have been influenced by *both* the mode of presentation and interaction with other jurors. Such confounding would make it impossible to isolate the impact of the alternative modes of presentation per se.

A second departure from normal trial procedures was necessitated by a statistical consideration. The tests used to analyze data collected during the studies required sample sizes greater than the typical six- or twelve-person jury. The needed sample size could be obtained either by reenacting the live trial several times or by using an abnormally large jury. The decision to use larger than normal juries was a calculated risk mandated by time and money constraints and by the realization that variability in the several reenactments of the trial was inevitable, no matter how skilled the performers. The participating judge opined that juror suspicion concerning the authenticity of the trials would be largely alleviated by an explanation from the bench. Although we were skeptical, we prepared a fictitious explanation concerning a Michigan State University-National Science Foundation research project investigating the effects of different jury sizes on verdicts rendered, and the judge gave the explanation to the jurors before the trial began. The success of this explanation and the realism of the trial reenactments are attested to by the fact that no juror ever expressed doubt about whether he or she was participating in an actual trial.

The procedures typically followed in these studies were as follows. On the day of the live trial, jurors were brought into the courtroom and seated in the spectator section facing the hearing area. The judge explained that the videotape recording cameras in the courtroom would be used to make a record of the trial for possible later appeal or review. Actually, the videotapes subsequently were used as stimuli in the videotape conditions. The judge further explained that the abnormally large jury size would allow a group of researchers from Michigan State University, who were interested in jury size, to analyze the results of the trial. The jurors were assured that they would determine the verdict in the case, and their decision would be binding on the litigants. Because of the large jury size, the judge explained, *voir dire* would be accomplished by means of a written questionnaire.

After *voir dire* questionnaires were completed by the jurors and the attorneys had examined them, four jurors were peremptorily dismissed, a tactic employed to heighten realism. The judge then commenced the trial and the videotaping began. All video technical personnel and control equipment were situated in the judge's chamber outside the view of the jurors. By videotaping the live trials, we ensured that jurors exposed to taped presentations viewed an identical reenactment of the trials; i.e., we guarded against presentational variation in the live and taped trials.

Samuel Brakel (1975) has raised several questions regarding research aimed at assessing the impact of video technology in the courtroom. In particular, he argues that research using simulations of the kind just described cannot provide answers concerning the comparability of live and videotaped trial presentations. Moreover, he contends that the failure to identify effects in no way implies their absence from the trial. Brakel puts it this way:

> There are two major, distinctive classes of problems with the present studies in the videotaped trials field — methodological and substantive. Some of these are inherent in the subject matter and probably cannot be resolved. Others, however, are eminently avoidable and appear to result from prejudgment of the issues or simple failure to think them through.
>
> The methodological problems center around an inability to get hold of comparable events, a problem exacerbated by the resort to simulation, which is used — but wrongly — to overcome the comparability problem. The substantive problems can be summed up by saying that the failure to anticipate effects or to find the few effects anticipated has led to the conclusion that there are no effects. The failure to comprehend or agree on the importance of effects found has resulted in the conclusion that the effects are unimportant. While the studies are not policy conclusive, to put it at its mildest, they tend to be presented and interpreted as if they were [p. 958].

Brakel contends that the use of simulations is a fatal strategy because the substance of the communication processes under study is lost. Furthermore, he argues that actors are incapable of conveying "subtle information...relating to the issues that figure prominently in a real trial — guilt, innocence, fault, credibility, veracity, objectivity, accuracy, persuasiveness" (pp. 958-959). Is there a unique set of behaviors exhibited by actual trial participants which are indicative of guilt, innocence, fault, credibility, veracity, objectivity, accuracy, and persuasiveness? We think it highly improbable that such unique behaviors exist unless trial participants experience some mysterious type of communication metamorphosis when they testify at a trial, a metamorphosis that significantly alters their behavior when compared to "testimony" provided in nonlegalistic contexts such as interpersonal relationships. In fairness to Brakel, there may be changes in communication behaviors attributable to the increased stress of the courtroom, but these would constitute differences in degree rather than kind.

In the studies reported here, careful attention was given to the intensity of behaviors exhibited by trial participants. Experienced attorneys and judges assisted in the development of the simulations and counseled the actors concerning typical behaviors of defendants, plaintiffs, and witnesses in similar trials. Although variations in behavioral intensity might be detectable by skilled trial judges and attorneys, they were not noticed by the actual jurors involved in our research. As we noted earlier, none of the jurors indicated they were aware that the trials were simulations.

Brakel's argument against simulations, if extended to its logical extreme, constitutes an indictment of education generally and law school education specifically. The educational process relies extensively on the use of simulations to teach. Such simulations demonstrate the application of principles and resulting effects in a manner intended to generalize to situations encountered outside of the classroom environment. "Mock trials" are an integral part of most law school curricula and provide developing legal practitioners with experience that supposedly generalizes to the actual courtroom environment. According to Brakel's logic, the communication processes at work in an actual trial would be absent in a mock trial; consequently, law students would be unable to learn techniques necessary to influence these processes — a major problem, if not a fatal educational error.

Brakel's criticisms would be more convincing if he provided evidence to support them. The following assertion illustrates this shortcoming:

> Perhaps simulating trials and videotaping them may yield some general data about videotaping, even it tells us nothing about the

impact of the medium on trials. But simulating trials to learn about videotape is a very cumbersome way to go about collecting data that in many instances already has been collected in simpler and more direct ways [p. 959].

Unfortunately, Brakel failed to cite any of this simpler research or to discuss its findings. If such data exist, it is difficult *not* to assume they produced results similar to our own. After all, any findings showing that juror responses to videotape deviate significantly from their responses to live trials would strongly support Brakel's antivideotape position.

## THE LIMITATIONS OF OUR RESEARCH

Our comments concerning Bermant et al.'s and Brakel's criticisms certainly are not intended to imply that our research findings are without limitations. Instead, a number of potential restrictions on generalizability deserve mention. For instance, the results may not be generalizable to criminal proceedings. Reenactments of civil trials and depositions were used as stimuli in most of our studies. Whether or not criminal trials would yield similar effects remains an open question. Moreover, a number of serious constitutional problems must be resolved before videotape can be used extensively in criminal proceedings (Armstrong, 1976).

Any policy implications of our findings naturally are limited to those dimensions of video technology examined. More research is required to assess fully the potential impact of various production techniques. The number of techniques that could be used include variations in lighting, camera panning, zooming, camera angles, and special effects — possibilities that far exceed the scope of our research. Because of time and cost constraints, the production techniques examined were those most frequently used by legal practitioners.

Finally, while actual jurors were used in the studies whenever possible, they were sometimes unavailable. Residents of nearby communities and students from Michigan State University were recruited to participate in our studies when actual jurors could not be obtained. These participants were asked to role-play jurors and to assume that their decisions would be binding upon contesting litigants. Actual jurors believed they were participating in real trials and consequently did not have to make this assumption. Role-playing jurors might have made different decisions than actual jurors because of varying assessments of the impact of their decisions. The former group were told the studies might be used by legal policy-makers to support change in the legal system; and since these changes could affect them, they were urged to participate wholeheartedly. As mentioned, the actual jurors believed their decisions would have an immediate impact upon the litigants.

The potential limitations to generalizability posed by role-playing jurors are greatest for findings of studies using university participants. Comparatively speaking, studies relying upon community participants are more generalizable than those based upon the responses of university participants, while the results from studies involving actual jurors are most generalizable. This ranking rests on the assumption that community participants are more demographically and attitudinally similar to actual jurors than are university students. Several writers (Colasanto and Sanders, 1976; Kessler, 1975) have underscored the dangers to generalization posed by using university student samples. The demographic characteristics of students differ markedly from typical jury panels. Furthermore, many college students are battle-scarred veterans who have participated in a number of research projects. Their knowledge and experience may result in radically different expectations concerning social science research.

One area where different expectations may arise concerns the use of research duplicity. Deception is commonly used by social science researchers to reduce the potential contaminating effects of demand characteristics (Orne, 1959, 1962). *Demand characteristics* are "the totality of cues which convey an experimental hypothesis to the subject and which become significant determinants of the subject's behavior" (Orne, 1962: 779). Orne contends that study participants are motivated to be "good research participants" by behaving consistently with investigators' hypotheses. If the demand characteristics are obvious enough to provide participants with a working knowledge of the hypotheses, subsequent verification may be attributable to the participants' desires to conform with the predictions of researchers rather than from differences in relevant experimental variables.

Differences in the amount of trial-related information retained by university participants and actual jurors have previously been observed. Several of our studies (Miller et al., 1975) investigated the effects of using live, color videotaped, and monochromatic videotaped testimony upon the amount of trial-related information retained by actual jurors exposed to the presentations. As discussed more fully in Chapter 4, the findings indicated that as the length of viewing time increases, videotaped testimony produces greater retention, suggesting that videotape may better hold juror attention. Moreover, this effect was somewhat more pronounced for monochromatic than for colored tape. Even though the absolute differences in average retention scores were not large, the fact that relatively small differences produced statistically significant results indicates that the observed effect was remarkably consistent for jurors in each of the presentational modes. Using the same color and monochromatic videotaped testimony and the same measuring instruments, similar data were collected from university participants. Their retention scores were significantly higher than those of the actual jurors, so high that statistical comparisons across groups were not possible.

These findings lend additional weight to the concern about using university participants in legal research. Two possible objections to this concern merit consideration. First, it might be argued that the data fail to demonstrate that systematically different results for university participants would not have been observed *if* the information retention measure had discriminated better. In other words, the data do not support an argument against the ecological validity of university participant retention scores; rather, they identify a need for more difficult retention tests for participants drawn from the university. This objection ignores the important fact that jurors who remember more trial-related information may behave differently during deliberation proceedings than jurors recalling less information. Specifically, their greater fund of information may influence their evaluation of arguments presented during jury deliberation and their actual verdicts. Moreover, the overall difference in retention scores is itself sufficient cause to question the generalizability of findings from studies employing university participants.

Second, the data from the university sample might be used to counter the charge that role-playing jurors are less motivated and involved than actual jurors. Even though the data can be interpreted in this manner, they can also be explained in terms of a pronounced discrepancy in level of education. At a minimum, Miller et al.'s demographic data indicate that the educational level of actual jurors is considerably less than that of college students; at a maximum, in the absence of data bearing directly on this possibility, it is reasonable to assume that college students generally are more intelligent than typical jury panels. Granting this cognitive advantage, it is dangerous to support inferences about involvement or motivation with information retention scores. It is possible that college students not particularly involved or motivated may be capable of scoring higher than actual jurors who are highly involved.

Information retention is not the only area where comparative data for university samples and samples of actual jurors have been obtained. In two instances (Miller et al., 1974; Miller et al., 1975), the distribution of verdicts for university participants and for actual jurors who viewed the same reenacted trials has been examined. Consistent with earlier findings (Simon and Mahan, 1971), the student jurors demonstrated a liberal bias in both trials; i.e., they found for the defendant more frequently than did actual jurors. There are at least two plausible explanations for this difference: first, since they are younger, students may possess more liberal social and judicial attitudes than actual jurors; second, because of their more extensive educational backgrounds, students may have a more sophisticated, complex definition of *reasonable doubt*. Regardless of the explanation provided, the fact remains that student verdicts differ from the judgments of actual jurors.

Given these data, one might ask why we employed university participants in five of our studies (see Table 2.1). Although it would be easy to echo the cry of poverty frequently voiced by social scientists, such an explanation would be only partially true. University students were relied upon when one or more of three differing sets of circumstances prevailed: (1) when actual jurors or community residents were not available; (2) when the nature of the experiment precluded the use of actual jurors and community residents were unavailable; and (3) when the focus of a specific study did not demand reliance upon actual jurors or community residents.

We strove to avoid using students in those studies whose ecological validity and generalizability would be adversely affected. Obviously, this was not always possible; however, many of the studies shared overlapping foci and to some degree represented modified replications. Consistent findings across these studies increased our confidence in our conclusions. Broadly speaking, our studies can be clustered into four different groups focusing upon differences in mode of presentation of trial-related material, the effects of inadmissible evidence upon juror behavior, the ability of jurors to detect deception across different modes of presentation, and the effects of several video production techniques on jurors.

As reflected in Table 2.1, none of the conclusions relating to any one of these four clusters is solely dependent upon findings derived from student samples. Actual jurors participated in two of the three studies concerned with alternative modes of presenting trial-related information. Two of the four studies focusing upon the effects of inadmissible evidence involved actual jurors, while a third relied upon community residents. It was extremely

**TABLE 2.1: Types of Participants Utilized in Various Studies**

|  | Actual Jurors | Community Participants | University Participants |
|---|---|---|---|
| Live vs. monochromatic videotaped trials | X |  |  |
| Live vs. color videotape vs. monochromatic videotape trials | X |  |  |
| Mode of presentation by witness type deposition study |  | X |  |
| Videotape testimony in live trial study | X |  |  |
| Inadmissible evidence: 0 through 6 instances | X |  |  |
| Inadmissible evidence: 0, 3, and 6 instances |  |  | X |
| Editing techniques study | X |  |  |
| Inadmissible evidence deliberation study |  | X |  |
| Detecting deception: monochromatic vs. color videotape |  | X | X |
| Detecting deception: live, monochromatic videotape, audiotape, and transcript |  |  | X |
| Full-screen vs. split-screen |  | X |  |
| Multicamera system vs. fixed camera |  | X |  |
| Camera shot study: closeup, medium, and long shots |  |  | X |

difficult for us to obtain actual jurors for our jury deliberation study because of the time required to complete it. There were no court jurisdictions available that could provide us with either the facilities or the number of jurors needed to complete this study. Nevertheless, content analysis of the videotaped deliberations clearly revealed that the community residents as role-playing jurors approached this task seriously, and none of them ever raised questions about being part of an experiment.

Since the study investigating various types of editing techniques relied upon actual jurors, problems of generalizability were minimized. This study also provided an indication of whether jurors refer to inadmissible testimony during deliberations.

Evaluation of deliberation proceedings was accomplished by including confederates in the juries without the knowledge of actual jurors. The confederates reported that two of the five juries who were exposed to the inadmissible evidence discussed it during the deliberation proceedings. Even though the amount of data from the actual jurors is limited, it supports the generalizability of the findings accruing from the community residents involved in the inadmissible evidence deliberation study.

Students comprised the primary sample in both of the detecting deception studies, although a community resident subsample was included in the first study. The degree of control deemed necessary for these two studies dictated procedurally complex designs which precluded the use of actual jurors. Because of the relative unavailability of community residents, we were forced to rely primarily upon students.

The extent to which the deception findings can be generalized to the trial process merits careful thought. Obviously, the stimuli used in both of these studies depart considerably from typical trial procedures. Using an actual deposition or trial transcript would have required individuals to role-play trial participants who either did or did not perjure themselves. We wanted to use procedures that led to actual lying so as to reduce potential threats to the generalizabilty of the findings.

Given our awareness of the problems associated with verdict and information retention measures when student samples are employed, these dependent measures were not used in either deception study. Both studies centered primarily on the relationship between alternative modes of presentation and accuracy in detecting deception. It seems reasonable to assume that persons, whether in or out of court, exhibit similar nonverbal behaviors when lying although intensity may vary drastically given differing situations and differing consequences if lying is detected. Stated differently, there is no reason to believe the nonverbal bvehaviors exhibited while lying in these studies would differ in kind from those exhibited by perjurers during a trial. On the other hand, the manifestations of these behaviors may have been less intense and consequently more difficult to detect.

There are three differences between the testimony provided by deceitful individuals in our studies and by witnesses who commit perjury. First, the people providing testimony in our studies were not subjected to the intense questioning typical of most courtroom trials. Second, they were not forced to respond to any form of cross-examination designed to identify weaknesses or inconsistencies in their testimony. Finally, these persons did not anticipate that other people might provide information that would impugn their testimony. These differences may have contributed to less intense nonverbal cues in our studies than would be exhibited by deceitful witnesses during a trial. To the extent that this is true, the generalizability of the findings from both studies is limited.

The use of both community resident and university student samples satisfied two different, but related concerns. It might be argued that community residents, who have more experience than their younger student counterparts, might be better detectors of deception: the former group probably has had more experience with deceitful individuals and therefore is more familiar with the nonverbal cues accompanying the act of lying. Conversely, an equally plausible argument suggests that students, who are generally more intelligent and hence perhaps more perceptive than the community residents, would be better at detecting deception. By sampling both groups in the first study, we were able to evaluate the merits of these two arguments.

The final group of studies examined the potential influence of various production techniques upon juror behaviors. Role-playing jurors, including students, were used exclusively in these studies because no actual jurors were available. Because of the moderate number of techniques examined and the nature of the samples used, findings from these three studies are inadequate for developing sound policy statements governing the use of video production techniques. Additional research employing actual jurors should focus upon a larger variety of production techniques. Our findings provide some strong indications concerning the effects of the techniques examined and are presented with these qualifiers in mind.

## SUMMING UP

This chapter has outlined several of the arguments presented against the ecological validity of social scientific research dealing with the trial and jury processes, and has detailed our critical analysis of them. Hopefully, our discussion of specific comments directed at our own studies provides a useful framework for evaluating the research discussed in this volume. Certainly, it is not our intent for the findings to be treated as policy conclusive, for such decisions hinge on a complex set of issues extending far beyond the province of our research.

In Chapter 3, we describe the preparation of the reenacted trial used in our first study in considerable detail. Upon reading this description, the reader will note the relevance of many of our decisions to issues raised in the present chapter.

# 3

# VIDEO OR LIVE: JUROR RESPONSES
# IN TRIALS

As mentioned in Chapter 1, our research has consistently focused on two potential uses of videotape in the courtroom: prerecording entire trials for presentation to juries and videotaping depositions for use in otherwise live trials. Both of these uses are explored in the studies described in this chapter.

## JUROR RESPONSES TO LIVE
## AND VIDEOTAPED TRIALS

Although we had no single set of rigorously derived theoretical expectations concerning what differences, if any, to expect in juror responses to live and videotaped trials, several lines of thinking suggested that it would be useful to examine this question. At a very global level, the writings of scholars such as McLuhan (1964) stress the hegemony of the medium itself as the primary message in communication transactions: McLuhan argues that the medium has a pervasive influence on the way persons process information and the perceptions they develop of the external world. To be sure, most of his insights concern potential differences between alternative media — e.g., print versus television — rather than possible variations in media-mediated as opposed to directly experienced events. Still, his ideas are provocative and do suggest that the addition of any intervening medium to a communication transaction may impact the way information is processed and judgments are formed.

At a less abstract level, the complexity of the stimulus field to which jurors are exposed is drastically reduced by the use of videotape. During a live trial, the juror may be attending to the verbal and nonverbal behaviors of the witness, the facial expressions of the judge or defendant, a conversation between one of the attorneys and his clients, the murmured remarks of spectators, the reactions of the juror seated next to him, or numerous other stimuli. Although we attempted to create a taping system that would capture much of this detail and richness, it seems inevitable that tape results in some reduction in the stimulus field of jurors.

The major problem, however, lies in specifying the extent and direction of differences, if any, that might occur in juror responses to live and videotaped trials. Suppose, for example, that we are correct in assuming that the complexity of the juror's stimulus field is reduced when videotape is used. How might such factors as the verdict itself, the amount of information jurors retain, their perceptions of the trial participants, and their interest and motivation in serving as a juror be influenced by this reduction? Plausible arguments can be made for either, or several, possible opposing outcomes. Consider, for instance, the question of information retention. At first glance, it may appear that restriction of the stimulus field should facilitate juror retention of information. From a distraction viewpoint, this assumption is warranted. The many competing stimuli present in a live trial may divert jurors from the testimony of witnesses, the questions of attorneys, or the rulings of the judge, thus reducing the amount of information retained. If this is the case, elimination of these distracting stimuli by means of videotape should produce better retention of information by jurors.

But consider the other side of the coin. From a motivational standpoint, the rich milieu of the live trial may do a better job of holding juror interest. Extensive viewing of a videotaped trial may become boring and monotonous, causing juror attention to lag. If so, and if interest is necessary for retention of information, we would anticipate that the live trial would lead to better retention of information by jurors.

Because of the numerous possible conflicting predictions that could be generated, this study was question-centered, rather than hypothesis-centered. Specifically, we investigated the following major questions:

(1) Are there differences in verdicts (attributions of negligence) between jurors exposed to live and videotaped trials?
(2) Among jurors finding for the plaintiff, are there differences in the amount of award between those viewing the live and the videotaped trials?
(3) Are there differences in perceptions of attorney credibility between jurors exposed to live and videotaped trials?
(4) Are there differences in retention of trial-related information between jurors exposed to live and videotaped trials?
(5) Are there differences in motivation and interest between jurors exposed to live and videotaped trials?

## Preparing, Reenacting, and Taping the Stimulus Trial

Some detail about the preparation and presentation of the stimulus trial is in order, since the trial used in this study was also employed in a later investigation of juror response to split-screen and full-screen taped presentations and in some of the research dealing with inadmissible testimony. Moreover, our procedures for this trial illustrate the characteristics of the simulations used in most of the studies.

### Selecting the Case

Since videotape has thus far been used more extensively in the civil than in the criminal arena, we elected, after consultation with legal adivsers, to use a civil case. Moreover, we sought a "typical" area of litigation — i.e., a type of case which is frequently heard — to ensure maximum generalizability of the findings. Although a relatively unique case or a contest between extremely prominent attorneys might have been more interesting, the relevance of the results to most everyday litigation would have been questionable.

Two types of civil litigation were considered: automobile injury cases and slip-and-fall actions. The major disadvantage of an automobile injury case seemed to lie in the fact that the increasing adoption of no-fault insurance would reduce the number of such cases brough to trial. Conversely, slip-and-fall cases posed two major problems: first, they are often of low interest to jurors; and second, because most slip-and-fall cases involve actions brought by an individual against an institution, there may be initial bias among many jurors hearing the case. Since we were advised that automobile injury cases would still be heard relatively frequently under conditions of no-fault insurance and since we could minimize the problems of low juror interest and initial juror bias by focusing on this area of civil litigation, we decided to use an automobile injury case for the stimulus trial.

Our next step was to select a specific case. Several criteria guided this selection:

(1) *The length of time required to try the case should not exceed three to four hours.* Because the trial was to be reenacted in the courtroom before actual jurors, this criterion took account of practical restrictions on the availability of courtroom facilities and the costs involved in paying jurors to participate in the research. Moreover, reenactment of a three-to-four-hour trial represented a theatrical undertaking of considerable magnitude, surpassing the typical running time for most television, motion picture, or stage productions.

(2) *The merits of the opposing parties' cases should be roughly comparable.* Obviously, we had no precise measure for equating the two cases; however, we felt a rough measure of comparability could be achieved by relying on the judgments of legal experts. Comparability of the arguments and evidence was

particularly important for later research dealing with inadmissible testimony, for if the merits of the cases were grossly disparate, the addition or deletion of inadmissible testimony would have little discernible impact on juror response.

(3) *The abilities of the contesting attorneys should be roughly comparable.* Here, too, it was impossible to assess the strength of the two attorneys precisely, particularly since we were using written trial transcripts which provided little evidence about the lawyers' presentation skills. The latter factor was not of great import, however, since in recreating the trial, we sought actors with comparable presentation skills for the attorney roles. Attorney comparability was particularly crucial for obtaining measures of the effects of mode of presentation on juror perceptions of attorney credibility.

Armed with these three criteria, we worked in conjunction with consultants from the University of Michigan Law School to select an automobile injury case. After examining over forty trial transcripts, a case tried in Iron Mountain, Michigan in 1968 (James and Ann Desmarais v. Frank Myefski) was chosen. The key issue of the case involved the question of contributory negligence on the part of the plaintiff.

### Editing the Transcript

For the most part, the structure and content of the transcript remained unedited. There were, however, three areas in which some editorial discretion was exercised.

First, the names of all participants in the trial were changed and Anglicized; thus in the edited version, James and Ann Desmarais v. Frank Myefski became James and Marjorie Nugent v. Frank Clark. Besides protecting the identities of the actual trial participants, this change enabled us to avoid any juror bias that might arise from the use of ethnic names.

Second, certain details of the trial were altered to conform with the 1973 reenaction date and to facilitate procuring visual exhibits. For instance, the original year and model of the plaintiffs' car was a 1962 Comet. In the edited version, the year and model were changed to a 1968 Chevrolet, both to make the situation more believable to the jurors and to enable us to use available pictures showing the kind of vehicle damage described in the trial.

Finally, in consultation with legal experts, we edited some of the dialogue to eliminate objectionable material not actually contested by the opposing attorney in the original trial and to ensure an equal number of objections by both attorneys. The edited transcript contained six objections by each of the attorneys, two sustained by the judge and four overruled. For each attorney, four of the objections concerned substantive matters — i.e., matters relating to the introduction of facts or opinions as evidence in the case — and two concerned procedural matters — i.e., matters relating to errors in trial procedure. This equalizing procedure made it possible to keep the merits of the two cases and the behavior of the two attorneys relatively comparable and to establish an identical baseline for the insertion of additional inadmissible testimony in that phase of the research.

*Preparing the Trial for Presentation*

Realizing that a realistic reenactment of the trial was essential to ecological validity, we contracted with Jerry Dahlmann of Oakland University to cast and direct the trial. This director was recommended because of previous work with research projects requiring dramatizations and because of his access to numerous professional actors and actresses from which to cast the trial. Save for the judge and the bailiff, who were played by 68th District Judge Dale Riker and Court Bailiff Lofton Carlton, all participants in the trial were professional actors or actresses.

Casting of participants was based not only on acting ability but also on age and physical appropriateness for the part. The result was a cast that looked and sounded remarkably "like" the roles they portrayed.

Each trial participant received a character sketch of the individual to be portrayed. During rehearsal, they were directed to avoid aping the style of television courtroom dramas such as "Perry Mason" or "The Defenders"; rather, they sought to develop their roles as "ordinary" persons who would usually be unsure, hesitant, and somewhat nonfluent in a trial setting. With the possible exception of the attorneys, whose presentation skills and audience impact probably exceeded that of the typical trial lawyer, the participants adapted to this style remarkably well and behaved quite similar to witnesses observed in actual trials. To some extent, the attorneys' eloquence is probably explained by the extent to which they entered into their roles; both had a strong competitive urge to best the other in trial combat.

For control purposes, all participants were required to learn their lines closely, thus avoiding ad libs and improvisation. This task was most onerous for the attorneys, who had to master a great deal of dialogue. Fortunately, it was possible to lighten their task by realistic use of notes on yellow legal pads. All participants learned their lines well, so that their dialogue conformed very faithfully to the edited transcript.

After studying lines for a week, the participants rehearsed for a week prior to the live trial reenactment. All rehearsals were held at the trial setting, the courtroom of Genesee County Circuit Judge Thomas Yeotis. Initial rehearsals were devoted to developing realistic blocking and movement that would not hinder unobtrusive videotaping and to practicing segments of the trial. Later rehearsals involved run-throughs of the entire trial. On the evening before the live trial, a dress rehearsal of the entire trial was held and a version of the trial containing six additional instances of inadmissible testimony was taped for future use in the studies dealing with deletion of inadmissible testimony.

## Taping the Trial

Before selecting the equipment system to be used in taping the trial, we reviewed and studied systems presently in use as well as those which had previously been proposed. Based on this review, we formulated a set of objectives appropriate to both an operational system and our experimental system:

(1) The videotaped material should be rich enough to hold the attention of the viewers.
(2) The videotaped material should allow all relevant participants to be seen, heard, and identified.
(3) The videotaping should be unobtrusive to minimize disruption of the court routine.
(4) The videotaping format should be static to avoid the possibility of editorializing.
(5) The system should be based on equipment equal in complexity and cost to the equipment most likely to be used in actual courtroom situations.

Given that some of these objectives were competing, we sought to select an equipment system that would optimize the objectives. Actually, the trial was eventually recorded using both a split-screen and full-screen taping system.

Based on the advice of our technical consultants, a split-screen system was devised to tape the trial. The split-screen technique involved partitioning the television screen so as to show three different perspectives simultaneously, closely akin to the techniques used to broadcast national sports events.

As designed, this system permitted the synchronous recording and playback of three shots on the same television screen. One shot was located in the lower half of the screen and showed the entire active area of the courtroom. The second shot was located in the upper left quarter of the screen and showed only a closeup of the witness in the witness box. The third shot was located in the upper right quarter of the screen and included only the bench and the questioning attorney. Figure 3.1 depicts the images seen by jurors on the television monitor.

Since the split-screen system was experimental, we felt a more conventional alternative system should be additionally developed to allow for secondary back-up recording and to create the potential for a subsequent study of the effects of the split-screen technique. For these reasons a full-screen taping

## Figure 3.1: SPLIT-SCREEN FORMAT

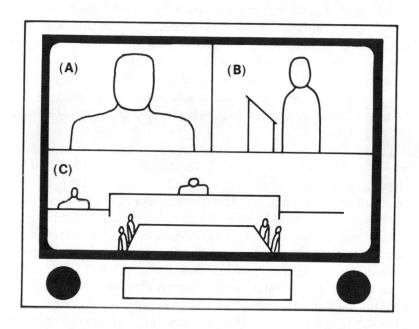

(A) **Close-up of witness**
(B) **Medium range shot of questioning attorney**
(C) **Full shot of courtroom excluding spectator area**

system was also employed. This system used a single camera and recorder to record one shot of the courtroom. The shot was the same view of the active area of the courtroom which appeared on the bottom half of the monitor in the split-screen version.

All equipment for both systems was chosen to equal the complexity and cost of equipment most likely to be used in actual courtroom situations. Videotape recorders were one-half inch monochromatic recorders which conformed to the conventional EIAJ standard. All playback was on conventional television sets as opposed to more expensive studio monitors. The cameras and the supporting video and audio equipment were of the variety commonly used in high schools and colleges for educational purposes.

To facilitate taping, the courtroom furniture arrangement was slightly modified (Figure 3.2). Lighting was provided by large draped windows along the right wall and indirect fluorescent lighting in the ceiling. The conditions for videotaping were generally comparable to those of an average courtroom.

Equipment was positioned as unobtrusively as possible given the constraints of the courtroom. All cameras used for both systems were placed on fixed, unmanned tripods. Two cameras were placed in the center of the courtroom along the rear wall, elevated on a small table. The two remaining cameras were placed seven to ten feet from the side walls immediately in front of the bar. The audio equipment permanently installed in the courtroom was used, with the addition of two microphones placed at the litigants' table. All videotape recorders, monitors, split-screen devices, and audio-mixing equipment were located in the judge's chambers behind the courtroom. At no time were personnel visible to the jury.

On the day of the trial, the jurors were brought into the courtroom with all equipment positioned and unmanned. After a brief fictitious explanation of why the equipment was present, the judge began the trial and the taping began. Four technicians manned the equipment in the judge's chambers and carried out continuous adjustments of both the video and audio components of the system.

# Figure 3.2: PHYSICAL LAYOUT OF COURTROOM

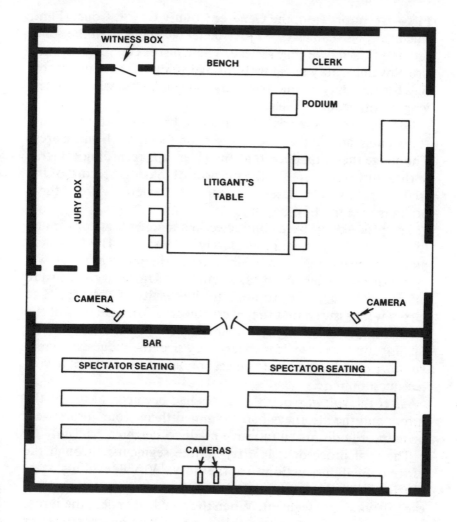

## Procedures

### Live Condition

Fifty-two jurors from the Genesee County Circuit Court (Flint, Michigan, November 1973) jury panel participated in the study on their final day of jury service. These jurors comprised the entire November jury panel with the exception of those not reporting for jury duty on that particular day and those who were serving on other jury panels.

On the day of the trial, jurors were brought into the courtroom and seated in the spectator section facing the hearing area. The judge then explained that the videotape recording cameras in the courtroom were for the purpose of making a record of the trial for possible later appeal or review. After these preliminaries the trial began.

The proceedings were conducted in a manner that conformed to normal trial procedure as closely as possible. The judge explained that the abnormally large size of the jury was to allow a group of researchers from Michigan State University, who were interested in jury size, to analyze the results of the trial. The jurors were assured that they were the actual determiners of the verdict in the case, and that their decision would be binding on the litigants. Because of the large jury size, the judge explained, *voir dire* questioning would be accomplished by means of a written questionnaire.

After the *voir dire* questionnaires had been completed by the jurors and the attorneys had examined them, four jurors were peremptorily dismissed (a move made to heighten realism).

The trial proceeded, in fifty-minute segments, through the judge's final instructions to the jury. Visual exhibits were distributed at the appropriate times. Recesses were taken after each fifty-minute segment. When the trial had ended, the jurors were taken to the jury assembly room, where an experimenter administered the "jury size" questionnaire. After completing the questionnaire, all jurors were completely debriefed. Little

suspicion about the reality of the trial was expressed either oral-
ly during the debriefing session or on the questionnaires. Jurors
did not deliberate, since, for purposes of this study, we were interested only in what jurors take to the jury room with them.
Questions involving deliberation are compelling and important,
but they were beyond the scope of the present research.

### Videotaped Condition

Participants were forty-five jurors from Genesee County who
viewed the videotaped trial on the last day of their jury service
one month later. The same research personnel were used, and
the two attorneys were again present to conduct an ostensible
written *voir dire* and to observe the trial. The single variation in
procedure was that the trial was viewed by jurors on six television monitors placed in the spectator section of the courtroom,
rather than being seen live. The judge's preliminary instructions
to the jury addressed this difference, explaining the split-screen
system and admonishing the jurors that, although the trial
would be viewed on television, it was fully as important as any
trial they had sat on during their term of jury service. Visual exhibits were distributed at the appropriate times. At the conclusion of closing arguments, the judge entered the courtroom and
read instructions to the jury.

As with the live presentation of the trial, jurors were taken to
the jury assembly room, where the experimenter administered
the "jury size" questionnaire. After completing the questionnaire, all jurors were completely debriefed. Again, little suspicion on the part of any juror about the unreality of the trial was
voiced or noted on the questionnaires.

### Measuring Instruments

In constructing the measuring instruments for this study, we
tried to create a highly structured but minimally complex set of
measures which would yield maximum information. The
criterion of maximum information was clearly necessary to
answer the five questions investigated. The simplicity and structure criteria represented an attempt to obtain data that would be

highly reliable, and therefore maximally generalizable to other jurors.

Both the verdict and the award measures were derived from the presiding judge's instructions to the jurors. In treating the negligence issue, the verdicts could have been broken down in several ways. We elected to classify them according to the legal criterion of liability. Thus, if a juror found the defendant, Frank Clark, solely negligent, we scored the response as a verdict for the plaintiffs; if a juror found Clark not negligent or found contributory negligence on the part of the plaintiff, Marjorie Nugent, we scored the response as a verdict for the defense. The jurors who found for the plaintiffs were then asked to specify an award for James Nugent (derivative action) and an award for Marjorie Nugent for pain and suffering. These awards, which could range from nothing to $3,136 for Mr Nugent and from nothing to $42,500 for Mrs Nugent, were used to determine the mean award for each of the two modes of trial presentation.

The perceived credibility of the attorneys was assessed with a set of fifteen semantic differential-type scales: five each for the competence, trustworthiness, and dynamism dimensions of credibility (Berlo et al., 1969-1970; McCroskey, 1966). The measure of each dimension of credibility was arrived at by summing across the five relevant scales; hence, a score of five reflected maximally unfavorable perceptions of credibility, while a score of thirty-five reflected maximally favorable perceptions.

The retention measure consisted of a forty-item examination, made up primarily of multiple-choice and true-false questions, but also containing some unaided, specific recall items. The questions used were selected from a larger item pool that was pretested with another group of persons and subjected to item analysis. Besides being the most reliable, the items chosen were distributed approximately equally over the duration of the trial.

Finally, the measurement of juror interest and motivation consisted of a set of eleven semantic differential-type scales. The mean interest and motivation score was derived by summing across the scales and dividing the total by eleven; consequently, a score of one represented minimal interest and motivation, while a score of seven reflected maximum interest and motivation.

## Results

Table 3.1 contains the breakdown of the negligence verdicts for jurors who viewed the live and the videotaped versions of the trial. Analysis of these data revealed no evidence that the mode of presentation significantly influenced juror attributions of negligence. Although jurors found for the plaintiffs somewhat more frequently in the videotaped trial condition — i.e, they found the defendant, Frank Clark, solely negligent with greater frequency — these differences do not approach significance ($x^2 = 2.55$, p. $>.10$).

The mean awards for both Mr and Mrs Nugent are also found in Table 3.1. In neither instance did the mode of presentation significantly affect the amount of award given by jurors who found for the plaintiffs; in fact, the comparisons across the two presentational conditions yielded small values $t = < 1$ for both Mr and Mrs Nugent's awards). While there is a difference of approximately $3,000 in the amount awarded Mrs Nugent by jurors in the live and videotaped trial conditions, that difference is more than offset by the substantial variability of awards given by jurors within each of the two conditions.

Juror perceptions of credibility were uniformly high for both attorneys but did not differ significantly across the two trial

### TABLE 3.1
**Negligence Verdicts and Mean Awards for Mr. and Mrs. Nugent by Jurors in the Live and Videotaped Trial Conditions**

|  | For Plaintiffs | For Defense | Mean Award Mr. Nugent | Mean Award Mrs. Nugent |
|---|---|---|---|---|
| Live trial | 13 | 31 | $2,761 | $20,538 |
| Tape trial | 20 | 21 | $2,660 | $17,975 |

conditions. Table 3.2 contains the mean competence, trustworthiness, and dynamism ratings for the plaintiffs' attorney and the attorney for the defense. We compared the ratings each of the attorneys received from the live trial and the videotaped trial jurors. None of these comparisons was significant. Thus, the mode of presentation did not influence juror perceptions of either attorney's credibility.

Likewise, in this study, juror retention of trial-related information was not significantly influenced by the medium of presentation. Of a possible score of 40, the mean retention score for jurors in the live trial condition was 31.1, while the score for jurors in the videotaped trial condition was 29.8. The resultant $t$ of 1.37 for the comparison of these means was not significant.

Finally, juror interest and motivation did not vary significantly as a result of watching a live or videotaped trial, a finding suggesting that there is nothing inherently less interesting or motivating about watching a videotaped trial rather than its live counterpart. The mean rating of interest and motivation for jurors in the live trial condition was 4.51, while the mean for jurors in the videotaped trial condition was 4.24 ($t = 1.12$). Since the midpoint on the scale used to measure juror interest and motivation is 3.50, it appears that both groups of jurors were moderately interested in, and motivated by, the task of jury service.

### TABLE 3.2
#### Ratings of Credibility for the Contesting Attorneys by Jurors in the Live and Videotaped Trial Conditions

|  | Plaintiffs' Attorney | | | Defense Attorney | | |
|---|---|---|---|---|---|---|
|  | Compe-tence | Trust | Dynamism | Compe-tence | Trust | Dynamism |
| Live trial | 28.22 | 26.16 | 26.96 | 29.16 | 26.65 | 28.41 |
| Tape trial | 27.02 | 26.18 | 25.91 | 28.17 | 26.67 | 27.67 |
| $t$ value | 1.11 | $<1$ | $<1$ | $<1$ | $<1$ | $<1$ |

In order to ascertain the relative comparability of the two groups of jurors, we examined their responses to a personal history the court had asked them to complete when they reported for jury duty. This form contained items dealing with such potentially relevant variables as age, sex, number of years of education, occupation, and prior jury experience. There were no significant differences between jurors who viewed the live and videotaped trials on any of these variables, and in most instances means and frequencies were highly comparable. Hence, the two groups of jurors manifest considerable homogeneity on personal and demographic characteristics which might influence their responses to the measures used in the study.

## Discussion

Results of this study reveal no detrimental effects on juror response as a function of viewing the videotaped trial. When compared to their live trial counterparts, jurors who watched the videotaped trial arrived at similar judgments, both in terms of verdict and amount of award recommended to the plaintiffs; reported similar perceptions of the credibility of the contesting attorneys; retained as much of the trial-related information; and reported similar levels of interest and motivation toward the task of serving as jurors. Moreover, numerous jurors with whom we visited expressed enthusiasm for the potential of videotape as a courtroom communication medium and indicated that in litigation of their own, they would prefer a videotaped to a live trial, a preference consistent with that expressed by a majority of the viewers in the Bermant et al (1975) study.

The absence of differences in ratings of attorney credibility for the live and videotaped trial conditions could be interpreted as reassurance for lawyers who fear that using videotape might lead to a reduction in their courtroom effectiveness. Such an interpretation must be offered cautiously. As previously mentioned, the courtroom communication skills of both attorneys probably exceeded those of the average trial lawyer. Both were actors with considerable experience in television and film media.

Whether this same degree of relative effectiveness holds for attorneys with limited media backgrounds remains a question for future research.

As with several of the other studies reported in this volume, this investigation primarily produced findings of no differences in juror responses to the live and videotaped trials. Stated statistically, we were unable to reject the null hypothesis for any of the five measures used in the study. Using a medium effect size ($n^2 = .06$), the results of power analyses (Cohen, 1969) for each of the dependent variables, save for the nominally scaled verdict award, revealed that in all cases the power associated with the test was greater than .75. This fact attests to the minimal likelihood of Type 2 error. Moreover, the realism and believability of our simulation bolsters our confidence in the findings. Unlike most previous research, we used actual jurors who viewed a complete trial in a courtroom setting. That these jurors responded similarly in the two conditions bodes well for the communicative comparability of the two presentational modes.

## JUROR RESPONSES TO VIDEOTAPED TESTIMONY IN A LIVE TRIAL

In the majority of instances, jurors do not watch an entire videotaped trial; rather, they see taped depositions of one or two witnesses while viewing the rest of the trial live. The utility of videotape used in this way hinges upon its capacity to present testimony without introducing bias. Unfortunately, there is reason to suspect that taping witnesses might influence the impact of their testimony.

Mass media researchers have long recognized the status-conferral function of media. Lazarsfeld and Merton (1952) note:

> enhanced status accrues to those who merely receive attention from the media. ...The mass media bestow prestige and enhance the authority of individuals and groups by *legitimizing their status*. Recognition (by the media) testifies that one has arrived, that one is important enough to have been singled out

from the large anonymous masses, that one's behavior and opinions are significant enough to require public notice [p. 76].

Since most people rely upon television for news, the status-conferral effect could conceivably be activated when a witness's testimony is presented on television monitors.

If this effect generalizes to the courtroom, then the presentation of a witness's testimony via videotape, as opposed to a live appearance, will enhance the perceived credibility of the witness. Mass media studies have consistently demonstrated that television is perceived as the most credible source of information (e.g., Greenberg and Roloff, 1974). This type of biasing effect might result in more favorable verdicts for the litigant for whom the videotaped witness testified.

Additional support for this line of reasoning arises from the novelty (from the jurors' perspective) associated with the use of videotaped testimony. Most jurors who participated in our research have never served on a jury before. Initially, we were surprised at this fact but have been repeatedly told by court officers, attorneys, and judges that this is quite normal. We are also increasingly convinced that juror expectations concerning trial process are significantly shaped by courtroom drama presented on television. Given these two factors, it is reasonable to assume that jurors expect witnesses to give live testimony and would be somewhat surprised to receive videotaped testimony. Stated more succinctly, jurors expecting witnesses to testify live will find videotaped presentations to be novel.

Wyer (1974) has demonstrated that novel information exerts more influence on message recipients than commonplace information (pp. 223-227). Furthermore, he suggests that novelty may increase attention to a given item of information relative to other information presented with it. If this effect exists, it should hold not only for novel information but also for information presented in a novel manner. Thus, videotaped testimony may exert greater influence on jurors than live presentations in a typical live trial.

Finally, there are numerous reasons for a witness to be absent. Especially when the witness is an expert in some field, a juror might reasonably conclude that the witness's appearance on videotape results from pressing business elsewhere; i.e., the witness is an *important* person with numerous commitments. Videotaped testimony would, therefore, have a disproportionate impact on a juror who had reasoned in this manner, since juror evaluation of the witness's expertise would be inflated.

All of the preceding considerations suggest that jurors may be unduly influenced by the appearance of videotaped testimony in an otherwise live trial. Our next study examines this possibility in a courtroom setting.

**Procedures**

We employed four treatments in which the medium of presentation for two expert trial witnesses was varied. In one condition both expert witnesses testified live under fairly typical court conditions. In a second condition the testimony of both expert witnesses was shown to jurors on monochromatic videotape. In a third condition the expert witness called by the plaintiff testified live, while the testimony of the expert witness called by the defendant was shown to jurors on black-and-white videotape. In the final condition the testimony of the expert witness called by the plaintiff was shown to jurors on black-and-white tape, while the expert witness called by the defendant testified live.

Participants were 106 Flint, Michigan, jurors drawn from the jury pool of the 68th District Court. The drawing was random for each of the four conditions. Since some jurors were unable to serve (for health reasons, having moved from the district, etc.) there were unequal numbers in the four conditions: 22 jurors in the live condition and 28 jurors in each of the remaining conditions.

Jurors were escorted to a courtroom which differed from the normal trial setting in two ways: there were far more than the usual number of jurors present and some videotape equipment was set up in the room. As in the preceding study, the judge's opening remarks stressed that this particular trial was being conducted in cooperation with a National Science Foundation study of jury size, thus providing an explanation for the large number of jurors. The judge explained that the camera would provide a record of the trial for the National Science Foundation researchers. He added that the case involved a change of venue, that because of its unusual circumstances the National Science Foundation had heard about it, and that they had secured an agreement with the litigants to research the case. These instructions not only explained the use of videotaped testimony — because of the change of venue the witness, or witnesses, could not be present — it also justified the fact that questionnaires were prepared in advance — this was possible becaue the NSF researchers had a great deal of knowledge of the case from working with the attorneys and the litigants. Finally, the judge ensured the jurors their decision would be binding upon the litigants.

The case involved an automobile accident in which the defendant admittedly was at fault. The point of contention concerned injuries. The plaintiff claimed that back injuries had been sustained as a result of the accident. The defendant claimed that the plaintiff's back problems were the result of a previous back condition, inadequate treatment, the plaintiff's negligence in following the instructions of the physician, and the plaintiff's weight problem. The trial's duration was approximately two hours and fifteen minutes.

The expert witnesses were two physicians, one who testified for the plaintiff and one who testified for the defendant. The other trial participants were the wife of the plaintiff — who was the person involved in the accident — two attorneys, and the judge. The former three participants were professional actors. The attorneys were played by a lawyer and a law school student. The judge was Dale A. Riker, 68th District Court Judge in Flint, Michigan.

When it was necessary to show videotaped testimony, the monitors were placed in clear view of the jurors. The videotape recorder was housed in a room behind the courtroom, and was out of sight of the jurors. The tape of the relevant testimony was made prior to the experiment.

Following presentation of the trial, the jurors were asked to fill out a questionnaire containing: (1) several measures of award, i.e., the minimum fair award, the maximum fair award, and the single most fair award; (2) measures of certainty, or confidence, in each of the award estimates; (3) a set of multiple choice items to measure the amount of trial-related information retained; (4) credibility measures for each of the trial participants which tapped the dimensions of sociability, extroversion, composure, competence, and character; and (5) measures of the salience of issues, and whether the issues favored the plaintiff or the defendant.

### Results

In assessing the impact of the mode of presenting witnesses, several dependent variables were examined. First, we considered the effect of mode of presentation on juror award. Table 3.3 contains the means, variances, and number of jurors for each of the four conditions. For both the defendant's expert witness and the plaintiff's expert witness, awards were higher (more favorable for the plaintiff) in the live presentation conditions. Nevertheless, results of an analysis of variance performed on these data show that neither of these main effects is statistically significant (F, plaintiff's witness = $<1$; F, defendant's witness = $1.14$, p. $>.05$). The strength of these effects was further assessed using the correlation ratio, and was found to be nonexistent ($n^2 = .00$ for the main effects and the interaction effect).

A note of caution in interpreting these data is appropriate. A high award may be interpreted as a relative success for the plaintiff and as a relative failure for the defendant; conversely, a low award may be interpreted as a relative failure for the plaintiff

## TABLE 3.3
### Mean Awards by Jurors Viewing the Four Versions of the Trial*

|  |  | Defendant's Witness<br>Live | Videotape |  |
|---|---|---|---|---|
| *Plaintiff's Witness* | Live | M = 3,728<br>s² = 4,584,823<br>N = 22 | M = 3,044<br>s² = 8,305,636<br>N = 28 | M = 3,386 |
|  | Videotape | M = 3,086<br>s² = 8,536,798<br>N = 28 | M = 2,642<br>s² = 6,963,635<br>N = 28 | M = 2,864 |
|  |  | M = 3,407 | M = 2,843 | M = 3,125 |

* Awards and variances are to nearest dollar amounts.


## TABLE 3.4
### Mean Retention Scores for Jurors Viewing the Four Versions of the Trial

|  |  | Defendant's Witness<br>Live | Videotape |  |
|---|---|---|---|---|
| *Plaintiff's Witness* | Live | M = 37.73<br>s² = 10.02<br>N = 22 | M = 32.93<br>s² = 27.40<br>N = 28 | M = 33.33 |
|  | Videotape | M = 30.39<br>s² = 38.36<br>N = 28 | M = 31.41<br>s² = 30.10<br>N = 27 | M = 30.90 |
|  |  | M = 32.06 | M = 32.17 | M = 32.12 |

and a relative success for the defendant. Hence, if the data presented in Table 3.3 are interpreted in this way, the two witnesses clearly are more effective given different modes of presentation; specifically, the plaintiff's witness helps his client obtain a more favorable verdict when appearing live, while the defendant's witness helps his client obtain a more favorable verdict when appearing on videotape.

The effect of mode of presentation upon the amount of trial-related information retained by jurors was also examined. Table 3.4 contains the descriptive statistics on information retention for each of the four conditions. Observation of this table suggests that more testimony was retained when the plaintiff's witness appeared live, rather than via the videotape medium. However, mode of presentation made little difference with respect to the defendant's witness.

The results of an analysis of variance confirm these observations. Although the effect of the mode of presenting the plaintiff's witness was statistically significant (F = 5.85, p < .05), it was not large ($n^2$ = .05). Certainly this effect is attenuated somewhat by the unreliability of the dependent measure ($r_{xx}$ = .80); however, it is more likely that the effect is small as a result of the nature of the information retention scale. This scale consisted of a variety of items designed to measure different types of information content: items pertained to information offered by the plaintiff, the plaintiff's attorney, the defendant, and the defendant's attorney. Perhaps if only the impact of the effect of mode of presentation on those items pertaining to the plaintiff's witness were considered, a large effect would be obtained.

To test this possibility, an analysis of variance was performed on only those sixteen items which measured juror retention of information presented by the plaintiff's witness. Once again, there was a statistically significant relationship between mode of presenting the plaintiff's witness and retention of the plaintiff's witness's testimony (F = 10.12, p < .05), such that more of this testimony was retained in the live presentation conditions. The strength of the relationship as measured by the correlation ratio is somewhat larger than was observed for total information retention ($n^2 = .09$); however, the effect is still not extremely strong. The unreliability of the dependent variable attenuates the estimated strength of effect, and in this case, there is considerably more unreliability than was measured in the total information retention scale ($r_{xx} = .64$). Correcting the correlation between mode of presenting the plaintiff's witness and retention of the plaintiff's witness's testimony results in a somewhat stronger estimated strength of relationship ($r = .38$).

It should be stressed that the same pattern was not observed when the ten items measuring retention of the defendant's witness's testimony were analyzed. The interaction of the mode of presentation of the two expert witnesses was the only significant effect observed ($F = 10.26$, $p < .05$). The form of this interaction indicates that more of the defendant's witness's testimony is retained when the witnesses are either both presented live or both presented on videotape, as compared to the conditions in which their testimony is presented via mixed modes. The strength of the interaction is weak; however, the defendant's witness's information retention scale is not very reliable ($r_{xx} = .50$). Correcting the correlation of the interaction term with the retention of the defendant's witness's testimony yields an $r$ of .20. This correlation, when corrected, is barely significant ($p = < .05$).

Once again, care should be taken in interpreting this outcome. Several points are noteworthy. First, the correlation is not particularly high, and it is only marginally significant. Moreover, it does not lend itself to a simple, intuitive explanation. Finally, since a considerable number of analyses were conducted, and since about 1/20 of the effects are expected to be significant by chance, this particular effect may reflect sampling error, rather than any actual relationship.

The relationship between mode of presentation of testimony provided by expert witnesses and juror perceptions of which of the litigants the evidence favored was also examined. The analysis of variance performed on these data failed to yield any statistically significant differences, or any effects of a large magnitude.

Finally, the influence of mode of presentation on source credibility was analyzed for each of the five trial participants. We will first consider the credibility of the plaintiff.

The mode of presenting expert witnesses significantly affected the credibility of the plaintiff ($F = 4.76$, $p < .05$), such that when the plaintiff's expert witness was presented live, the plaintiff was perceived as being more credible. While significant, this effect was not extremely strong ($n^2 = .05$).

Since credibility has repeatedly been shown to be a multidimensional concept, it is possible that the effect of the mode of witness presentation is restricted to one or two of the dimensions of credibility (e.g., Berlo et al., 1969-1970). In general, analysis of the credibility ratings by dimensions supports this possibility. In the live conditions, the plaintiff was perceived as being of higher character ($F = 6.49$, $p < .05$) than in the videotape conditions. Once again, the strength of the effect was not large, although it was a bit larger than the effect for overall credibility ($n^2 = .06$). Correcting this relationship for unreliability in the dependent variable does not increase the magnitude of the relationship to a great extent ($r = .27$).

Analysis of the impact of mode of presentation on the perceived credibility of the plaintiff's attorney yielded no significant differences. However, analyses of the effects of mode of presentation on the credibility of the plaintiff's witness produced several significant findings. The plaintiff's witness was perceived as being significantly more sociable ($F = 6.96$, $p < .05$), competent ($F = 13.10$, $p < .05$), of higher character ($F = 6.23$, $p < .05$), and generally more credible ($F = 12.40$, $p < .05$) when presented live as opposed to when presented on videotape.

The strength of these relationships varies across the multiple dimensions of credibility. With respect to the sociability of the plaintiff's witness, the correlation ratio indicates a rather weak relationship ($n^2 = .06$, r $= .25$). Correcting for the unreliability in the dependent variable fails to increase the estimated magnitude of relationship drastically (r $= .28$).

Mode of presentation also is weakly related to the character dimension of credibility ($n^2 = .06$, r $= .25$). Since the character dimension was found to be highly reliable ($r_{xx} = .92$) correction for attenuation had little effect on the correlation (r $= .26$).

The relationship between mode of presentation and competence is considerably stronger ($n^2 = .11$, r $= .35$). Since reliability is low for the competence measure ($r_{xx} = .51$), the correction for attenuation produces a large increase in the correlation (r $= .49$).

Mode of presentation is also strongly related to the total credibility score ($n^2 = .11$, r $= .34$). There is considerably less unreliability in the credibility measure ($r_{xx} = .82$); hence, in the correlation between these two measures (r $= .37$).

Finally, the effect of mode of presentation on juror perceptions of source credibility of the remaining two sources, the defendant's attorney and the defendant's expert witness, produced no significant differences.

## Discussion

Findings of this study reveal that the mode of presenting witnesses significantly affects three variables: juror awards, information retention, and source credibility. The nature of these effects, however, is not simple. For example, the plaintiff's witness was more effective in obtaining favorable awards for the plaintiff when he appeared live, whereas the defendant's witness was more effective when he appeared on videotape. In addition, while more of the plaintiff's witness's testimony was retained by jurors in the live conditions, mode of presentation did not exert a significant impact on the defendant's witness's testimony. Finally, both the plaintiff and the plaintiff's witness were perceived as being considerably more credible when the plaintiff's witness was presented live, but similar results were not obtained for any of the three other trial participants. In short, not only are the obtained effects in a direction opposite to those predicted, but they are also not consistent across sources.

Given these results, we are led to the conclusion that any impact of mode of presentation is strongly tempered by the communicative characteristics of individual witnesses. Apparently, different witnesses possess communication styles that are perceived differently depending upon the medium by which the witness is presented. In this study, we made no attempt to measure such witness characteristics. Moreover, the nature of these individual differences does not emerge clearly from viewing trial tapes.

After performing a number of analyses, then, we are left with the following commonsense generalization: *the relative impact of a given presentation mode is highly dependent on the ability of the particular communicator to use that mode.* Stated differently, it is doubtful that videotaped testimony per se will exert a disproportionate positive impact on jurors when inserted into an otherwise live trial. What is likely to occur are mode of presentation by witness interactions, such that one witness will be more effective live and another will be more influential on tape. Given this kind of conjunctive relationship, it will sometimes be disadvantageous (as indeed it was for the plaintiff's witness in this study) for a lawyer to introduce taped testimony into the trial; while on other occasions, using tape will be advantageous. Nevertheless, the advantage does not seem to accrue from any inherent persuasive power of the videotape medium but rather from the fact that a particular witness "comes across better" on tape than in a live setting.

## SUMMING UP

This chapter has described two studies dealing with juror responses to alternative modes of presenting trials and testimony. In neither study did the use of videotaped trial materials produce marked differences in the information processing or decision-making of individual jurors. When we compared responses of jurors who viewed the live and videotaped trial, no differences were observed on any of the five measures. Although some variations in juror respose did emerge in the study dealing with introducing taped testimony into a live trial, they appeared to be largely a function of the characteristics of particular witnesses, rather than resulting from the influence of the presentation medium per se.

Despite the apparent comparability of live and videotaped courtroom presentations, we conducted additional research dealing primarily with the effect of presentation mode on juror retention of trial-related information. Our next chapter reports the results of two studies which focused on this question.

*4*

# HOW MUCH DO JURORS REMEMBER?:
# VIDEO vs. LIVE TESTIMONY

At least two considerations motivated us to investigate further
the possible influence of presentation mode on juror retention
even though our earlier study comparing a live and videotaped
trial had yielded no significant differences on this dimension of
juror behavior. One involved certain theoretical expectations,
which we shall turn to momentarily. A second, more practical
consideration lay in the fact that retention of trial-related information provides a more meaningful baseline for assessing the
relative utility of live and videotaped trial materials than do
some of the other measures employed in our studies. Suppose,
for instance, that we were to observe a difference between the
two media on the pattern of verdicts rendered by jurors or the
magnitude of awards recommended for the plaintiff: e.g., suppose jurors watching the live trial found more frequently for the
plaintiff while their counterparts viewing the videotaped trial
found more frequently for the defendant. Since trial verdicts are
inherently probabilistic and judgmental — i.e., since no

foolproof way exists for arriving at the "correct" verdict — the legal implications of our hypothetical difference would have to be interpreted primarily on the basis of ideological bias. Persons of a liberal bias — i.e., those who would prefer erring more frequently in the directon of exonerating the defendant — would probably argue that wider use of videotaped trial materials is justified by our hypothetical finding, while persons of a conservative bent — i.e., those who would prefer erring more frequently in the direction of finding the defendant legally liable — would probably opt for the superiority of live presentation.

By contrast, a measure such as retention of trial-related information offers an objective baseline for evaluating the impact of the different presentation modes: the correct answers to factual questions about the trial can be ascertained and the retention levels of jurors exposed to the various modes can be compared. Moreover, since most jurists and legal experts subscribe to the value that trial outcomes should hinge primarily on the merits of the arguments and evidence presented, the legal implications of any differences in retention can be interpreted relatively unambiguously. Specifically, if jurors viewing videotaped trial materials retain as much as, or more information than jurors watching a live presentation, this outcome speaks positively for wider use of videotaped testimony in courtroom trials. On the other hand, lower retention scores for the former group of jurors would testify against extensive use of videotaped trial materials.

## PATTERNS OF INFORMATION RETENTION ACROSS PRESENTATION MODES

Even if the total amount of trial-related information retained does not differ markedly, the pattern of information retention for jurors viewing live, monochromatic, and color modes of presentation may differ over time because of differences in the patterns of retention between the three groups. Research by Miller and Campbell (1959) indicates that if people are interested in a communication, they will remember the last portion of the message to a greater extent than the first part. Conversely, if their interest is low, their recall of the first part will be better than their recall of later segments, presumably because these later segments are tuned out. Such differences could occur when testimony is presented to jurors via various presentation modes. Specifically, if one mode of presentation results in more personal involvement and interest for jurors than another, we would expect the jurors viewing the more involving presentation to remember the most recent information better.

Moreover, there are empirical grounds for assuming that jurors who view monochromatic and color videotaped testimony may differ in their patterns of information retention. Previous research (Kumata, 1960; Katzman, 1971; Schaps and Guest, 1968) provides evidence that viewers exposed to black-and-white television programs manifest information-processing patterns which differ from the pattern of color program viewers. Color presentations apparently result in greater retention of peripheral information, whereas black-and-white seems to produce better retention of central concepts and important information. To the extent that these findings hold for jurors viewing testimony, they suggest some potential differences in juror retention patterns depending upon the particular mode used to present witnesses.

Taken together, the preceding considerations led to a study designed to answer the following two questions:

(1) Are there differences in the amount or pattern of trial-related information retained by jurors exposed to live testimony and jurors exposed to videotaped testimony?

(2) Are there differences in the amount or pattern of trial-related information retained by jurors exposed to monochromatic videotaped testimony and jurors exposed to color videotaped testimony?

## Procedures

Thirty-one jurors from the 68th District Court, Flint, Michigan, were told by the presiding judge that they were viewing an actual trial. To justify the large jury, they were also told that the parties involved had agreed to participate in a jury size study, the same cover story used in the studies described in Chapter 3. Finally, the jurors were told the litigants had agreed that the trial could be halted from time to time to give the researchers on jury size a chance to administer questionnaires to jurors. Jurors were assured that despite these departures from normal trial procedures their verdict would be binding.

The jurors then viewed a live reenactment of the opening two hours of a will contest case. These two hours contained fifty-two minutes of testimony by the defendant, an attorney accused of exerting undue influence on a client so as to induce him to make the attorney's fraternal organization the major beneficiary of his will. Once again, the reenactment was based on an actual case, selected on the advice of legal experts, and was reenacted by professional actors save for the judge and bailiff, who portrayed themselves. The live reenactment was unobtrusively taped with color cameras for later use in the two videotape conditions.

After viewing the first two hours of the trial, the jurors completed a questionnaire which measured their retention of the defendant's fifty-two minutes of testimony. This segment was chosen to avoid confusing effects on test results stemming from varying delivery styles and possible differences in credibility that would occur with two or more witnesses. While jurors were filling out the questionnaires, they harbored the impression the trial would resume when they were done. Upon finishing the questionnaire, they were debriefed and dismissed.

In order to construct the questionnaire, we divided the fifty-two minutes of testimony into four thirteen-minute segments and developed an equal number of retention items (ten) for each segment. The resulting forty-item inventory permitted analysis not only of total retention by jurors but also of possible differences in retention curves over the fifty-two minutes of testimony.

The videotape of the reenactment was shown in color and black-and-white respectively to two other groups of thirty-one 68th District jurors. The judge appeared in the courtroom prior to the videotape showings and instructed the jurors that they were viewing a videotape of a trial where both parties had agreed to accept the judgment of the jury. The jury size cover story was again used. After watching the appropriate tape, jurors completed the retention instrument under the same conditions as jurors who had viewed the live trial.

## Results

Table 4.1 summarizes the mean retention scores across the four thirteen-minute time intervals for jurors who viewed the live, monochromatic, and color presentations. For all three presentation modes, retention of trial-related information was highest for the first thirteen minutes and declined significantly throughout the presentation ($F = 5.86$, $p < .05$). If Miller and Campbell's (1959) reasoning about order effects is correct, this finding suggests that most jurors found the trial relatively uninteresting.

The most important finding, however, was revealed by a treatment by time interval analysis of the retention curves for jurors exposed to the three modes of presentation. More rapid decline in retention occurred among jurors who watched the live testimony ($F = 6.34, < .05$). Jurors who viewed the two videotaped presentations retained more information from later segments of the testimony, with retention somewhat better for those watching black-and-white testimony.

## TABLE 4.1
**Mean Scores for Retention of Trial-Related Information by Jurors Viewing the Three Modes of Presentation**

|  | Mean Retention | | | | |
|---|---|---|---|---|---|
|  | Interval 1 | Interval 2 | Interval 3 | Interval 4 | Intervals 1-4 |
| Live | 9.8 | 8.3 | 7.7 | 7.6 | 8.3 |
| Black-and-white | 9.4 | 9.2 | 7.8 | 8.0 | 8.6 |
| Color | 9.0 | 8.6 | 8.5 | 7.8 | 8.5 |

To examine this latter possibility further, we conducted a secondary analysis in which monochromatic and color information retention scores were collapsed into a single video category and compared with the live trial group. This analysis produced no significant interaction between mode of presentation and time interval, lending credence to the suggestion that the monochromatic presentation led to the best retention of information presented in later segments of the testimony.

While the information retention patterns differ among the three modes of presentation, the absolute differences in mean retention scores are not large. This fact might lead some to contend that the differences, although statistically significant, are not great enough to exert any appreciable impact on the trial process. Two considerations are relevant when evaluating this argument. First, the study examined retention of trial-related information for only a single hour of testimony. To the extent that the observed differences in retention persist over longer time periods, the cumulative effect of a videotape presentation on juror knowledge could be considerable for a lengthy trial. Second, the fact that such small mean differences in retention scores produced statistically significant results indicates that the effect was remarkably consistent for the jurors in a given presentation.

### Discussion

In terms of its potential for communicating information effectively to jurors, the findings of this study support the efficacy of videotaped trial materials in comparison to the traditional live mode of presentation. Although the differences were certainly not large, jurors who watched the videotaped witness retained more information from later portions of his testimony. This outcome suggests that jurors were more interested and involved in the taped testimony than in the same information presented live (Miller and Campbell, 1959).

Unfortunately, the design of this study does not provide an unambiguous explanation as to why patterns of retention of trial-related information differed between jurors exposed to the three presentation modes. We tend to favor a *reduction of stimulus complexity* explanation. By virtue of the amount of information it provides, the live milieu is most complex and thus introduces the greatest number of potentially distracting stimuli. By committing the testimony to colored videotape, some of these distractions are eliminated, though the color mode still provides considerable peripheral information. Monochromatic taping screens out even more of these peripheral cues, allowing jurors to concentrate more closely on important evidence and argument. Since our retention test sought to tap these central facts and concepts, variations in retention patterns over time would be expected to favor the taped presentations, particularly the one presented monochromatically. Indeed, extension of our reasoning suggests that audiotape or transcript presentations might yield even higher retention, though we have no data pertaining to this possibility.

Appealing as this interpretation may be, its speculativeness must be emphasized, and the availability of alternative explanations must be granted. The most disquieting possibility is that over time differences in retention are but an ephemeral phenomenon resulting from the novelty of viewing testimony on videotape, rather than live. If so, our earlier argument can be reversed quite nicely by opponents or skeptics of the courtroom use of videotape. Whereas we suggested that differences in retention might have been more marked had the testimony been longer, a novelty interpretation leads to the opposite conclusion: as jurors watch larger amounts of videotaped testimony, interest associated with this initially novel form of presenting witnesses wanes and differences in retention of trial-related information are erased. Although we believe something other than sheer novelty is operating, we cannot be confident of our belief until further research has identified the precise antecedent factors that give rise to the observed variations in retention patterns.

The fact that monochromatic tape produced somewhat better retention of the later portions of testimony than did color tape implies that nothing is lost — and indeed, something may be gained — in juror retention by employing black-and-white taping systems, rather than their more expensive color counterparts. Still, differences in the two tape modes are not robust enough to inspire confidence in this conclusion. With this thought in mind, we carried out a second study designed to shed more light on possible differences in juror retention of trial-related information resulting from exposure to monochromatic and color taped testimony.

## JUROR INFORMATION RETENTION ACROSS TAPED MODES

The major objective of this study was to pursue further the possible relationship between the kind of taped presentation (monochromatic versus colored) and subsequent juror retention of trial-related information. In addition, we varied the communication skills of the witness (strong versus weak witness) to investigate potential interactions between this variable and the mode of presenting testimony.

As previously noted, the preceding study revealed that jurors remembered more of the later portions of testimony when they viewed witnesses on monochromatic, rather than color tape. Since jurors were tested for recall of important facts and evidence, this superiority is consistent with the findings of a prior study by Katzman (1971), who found that a color presentation results in greater retention of peripheral information while black-and-white tape produces greater recall of central information and concepts. Our reasoning, developed above, attributes this difference in information processing to the varying complexity of the two presentational modes: because it highlights peripheral information to a greater extent, color tape would be expected to confer cue properties (Miller and Dollard, 1941) on such incidental information, leading to better recall of this material by viewers watching color presentations. By contrast, monochromatic tape reduces the cue properties of such stimuli by filtering them out and/or reducing their distinctiveness, thus allowing viewers to attend more closely to the major information thrusts of the message. Armed with this reasoning and the results of prior research, we tested the following hypothesis:

(1) Jurors who view monochromatic testimony will retain more trial-related information than jurors who watch the same testimony on color tape.

To some extent, however, this hypothesized relationship may be affected by the communication skills of the witness. Given a skilled witness — i.e., one who delivers testimony in a rhetorically effective manner — the added information provided by color may emphasize, or reinforce, the important points of the testimony. Conversely, the communication ineptitude of a weak witness, as manifested in distracting paralinguistic and bodily mannerisms, should be further highlighted by color, suggesting that such a witness would fare better on black-and-white tape. These differences led to the following hypothesis, which posits an interaction between the relative communication skills of the witness and the mode of presenting testimony:

(2) The effect hypothesized in (1) will be greater for a weak witness than for a strong witness.

Finally, we tested two hypotheses concerning jurors' responses to the two types of witnesses:

(3) Jurors who view the testimony of the strong witness will retain more trial-related information than jurors who view the testimony of the weak witness.

(4) Jurors will perceive the strong witness as more credible than the weak witness.

**Procedures**

Because of the unavailability of a courtroom and actual

jurors, 117 adult Lansing residents were paid to participate in this study. Although not actually on jury duty, the demographic characteristics of these participants were quite similar to those of actual jurors used in previous studies. The participants were instructed to assume the role of jurors and were asked to approach the task seriously, since the results would be used to reach decisions about possible important changes in future trial procedures.

The videotape used was a reenactment of an actual deposition taken from an industrial accident case. A professional actor played the role of the witness, a truck driver who had been involved in the accident. Questioning was handled by two actual attorneys. The manipulation of witness type was achieved by having the actor play two different roles. In the strong witness role, he was assertive, attentive, confident, and unhesitant when giving testimony. In the weak witness role he exhibited paralinguistic and bodily behaviors to suggest that he was uncertain, inattentive, fumbling, and hesitant. The content of the testimony was identical for both presentations.

After the two versions were committed to tape, they were pretested to determine the success of the manipulation. Twenty-six Michigan State University undergraduates were shown twelve-minute excerpts from the beginning of each tape and were asked to rank order the tapes according to how strong, assertive, and confident the witness appeared to be. In all twenty-six instances, the tapes were ranked in the correct order, attesting to the efficacy of the manipulation.

The role-playing jurors were randomly assigned to one of the four conditions, and reported in groups on four consecutive evenings. Following a brief introduction of the study, the jurors viewed the appropriate version of the videotaped deposition: specifically, each group of jurors saw the testimony of either the strong or weak witness presented on either monochromatic or color tape.

After viewing the tape, the jurors completed a questionnaire designed to measure their information retention and their perceptions of the witness's credibility. Fifty-nine items, culled through prior item analysis, were used to index information retention; and sixteen semantic differential-type scales (Berlo et al., 1969-1970; McCroskey, 1966) were employed to assess witness credibility. When they had finished the questionnaire, participants were debriefed and dismissed.

## Results

Table 4.2 contains the mean retention scores for role-playing jurors who viewed the four different versions of the testimony. The scores are consistent with the differences posited in Hypothesis 1; i.e., role-playing jurors who viewed the testimony on monochromatic tape retained more of the trial-related information, regardless of whether it was presented by the strong or weak witness. A subsequent analysis of variance revealed that this effect was significant ($F = 6.55$, $p < .05$), thus confirming the hypothesis that jurors would retain more trial-related information if it were presented in black-and-white, rather than color.

Similarly, the analysis confirmed Hypothesis 3: role-playing jurors who watched the strong witness retained significantly more information across both modes of presentation ($F = 6.58$, $p < .05$) than did their counterparts who viewed the weak witness. This commonsense outcome is of limited substantive interest, but does provide yet another check of the effectiveness of our witness manipulation, since jurors would generally be expected to retain more testimony given by skilled than by unskilled witnesses.

**TABLE 4.2**
**Mean Retention Scores for Role-Playing Jurors**
**in the Four Conditions**

| Type of Witness | Mode of Presentation | |
| --- | --- | --- |
| | Black-and-white | Color |
| Strong | 39.72 | 34.59 |
| Weak | 36.17 | 33.31 |

The interaction posited in Hypothesis 2 was not supported by the analysis ($F = < 1$, $p < .05$). Moreover, while the interaction does not approach significance, its pattern is opposite to that predicted by Hypothesis 2: whereas the retention scores for role-playing jurors exposed to the weak witness are only 2.86 items greater in the monochromatic condition, they are 5.13 items greater for jurors who viewed the strong witness. Apparently, communicating testimony skillfully does not enhance the retention capabilities of the color medium; rather, the increased retention of trial-related information resulting from black-and-white presentation holds equally for both types of witnesses.

The juror ratings of witness credibility are found in Table 4.3. Consistent with the manipulation used in the study, the strong witness was perceived as significantly more credible than the weak witness ($F = 9.19$, $p < .05$). Although both types of witnesses were perceived as significantly more credible when viewed on color tape, the effect is more pronounced for the strong witness ($F$ for interaction $= 6.95$, $p < .05$). Thus, mode of presentation does not influence juror perceptions of credibility comparably for witnesses of varying communicative skills; for while both types of witnesses were perceived as more credible on color tape, the strong witness reaped greater credibility benefits from appearing in color.

## Discussion

The results of this study support the hypothesis that jurors will remember more trial-related information when it is presented on monochromatic, rather than color tape.

### TABLE 4.3
### Mean Ratings of Perceived Witness Credibility for Jurors in the Four Groups

| Type of Witness | Mode of Presentation | |
|-----------------|----------------------|-------|
|                 | Black-and-white      | Color |
| Strong          | 67.66                | 75.10 |
| Weak            | 63.80                | 64.63 |

Moreover, this effect is not mediated by the communicative skills of the witness, since the black-and-white testimony produced greater juror retention for both strong and weak witnesses. When combined with the outcomes of our prior information retention study, the findings lead to the following tentative conclusions concerning juror retention of trial-related information presented via live and taped depositions: (1) jurors remember as much total testimony presented on tape as they do testimony presented in a live setting; (2) jurors watching taped depositions remember more of the later portions of the testimony than jurors viewing the same testimony live, with this effect somewhat more pronounced for monochromatic than for color tape; and (3) jurors viewing testimony on monochromatic tape remember more of it than jurors who watch the testimony in color, with this effect holding for both skilled and unskilled witnesses. Naturally, these conclusions only pertain to central facts, evidence, and arguments; the kind of information tested for in the two studies.

We must reemphasize our uncertainty about the precise factors triggering these differences in information processing. Whether they stem from differences in stimulus complexity, format novelty, greater juror familiarity with television than the live medium (after all, many members of our society probably spend more hours per day processing information gained from television than from messages communicated in live settings), or yet other antecedent considerations remains a problem for future research. Regardless of the triggering mechanism(s), it appears that the use of taped testimony does not lead to a decline in juror retention of trial-related information; if anything, tape enhances retention. Moreover, as noted earlier, less expensive monochromatic taping systems produce better retention than more costly color systems.

When we turn to juror perceptions of witness credibility, however, the evidence shifts to favor the color medium. Both witnesses are rated more credible when seen in color, rather than black-and-white, though the effect is decidedly more marked for the strong witness. This finding suggests that an important portion of the information which jurors use in making credibility assessments is nonverbal. If so, much of this information might not be received from monochromatic tape; either because, as in the case of flushed skin, such information cannot be conveyed by a noncolor medium or because jurors do not attend as closely to the less interesting black-and-white visual display, thus missing the nonverbal signals upon which credibility judgments are at least partially based.

Taken together, the results of this study pose a perplexing and paradoxical problem for legal policy-makers. Apparently, the monochromatic mode yields better retention of trial-related information, while the color medium produces more favorable perceptions of witness credibility. Stated differently, the color format may magnify the importance of *image* at the expense of *information*, while the black-and-white format may enhance information retention at the cost of eliminating nonverbal cues typically used by jurors for assessing witness demeanor. If so, policy-makers will be forced to decide which of these juror response dimensions merits priority. Some additional evidence for making this decision will be presented in Chapter 7, when we present our research dealing with people's ability to detect deceptive testimony.

## SUMMING UP

This chapter has described the findings of two studies which sought to determine the influence of presentation mode on juror retention of trial-related information. Neither study revealed any detrimental influence on juror retention of trial-related information resulting from the use of taped, rather than live testimony. To the contrary, we concluded that jurors remember more of the later portions of testimony when it is presented on tape. In addition, jurors viewing testimony on monochromatic tape recall a greater amount of testimony than jurors watching the same testimony in color, regardless of the presentational skills of the witness. Thus, in terms of information retention, the verdict concerning use of videotaped trial materials is generally positive.

# 5

# OBJECTION SUSTAINED: DELETION OF INADMISSIBLE MATERIAL

As noted in Chapter 1, proponents of wider adoption of videotaped trial materials contend that one important advantage accruing from this courtroom innovation lies in the capability of deleting inadmissible, rule-violating material before jurors are exposed to it. This advantage stems from the asumption that jurors *cannot* ignore such material in arriving at a decision, even though the judge may admonish them to disregard it. In addition, these advocates argue that two other advantages would be realized by expunging inadmissible material: first, trial time would be substantially reduced; second, the process of ruling on objectionable material out-of-court would permit judges to ponder and research their rulings more carefully, thus lightening appellate court loads by reducing the number of reversible decisions. While the latter two advantages, if realized, have significant legal implications, our research has dealt primarily with the possible benefit of deleting inadmissible material before jurors are exposed to it; i.e., we have concentrated on determining whether juror verdicts and/or perceptions of attorney credibility are influenced by exposure to objectionable trial material.

The potential effects of infractions of evidentiary rules upon jurors have received considerable attention from social scientists. Wanamaker (1937) found that jurors responding to a questionnaire had discussed issues during deliberation that by law should not have been discussed. His findings, however, did not demonstrate that these discussions altered trial outcomes.

Weld and Danzig (1940) exposed two juries composed of persons known to have anti-Nazi sentiments to information indicating that an individual in a trial reenactment had pro-Nazi sympathies. Only one person mentioned this information during deliberation, and he was reminded by another juror of the judge's instructions to disregard the information. This study, however, included only two juries, far too few to permit meaningful inferences. Furthermore, the objectionable evidence was not very important within the trial context which dealt with civil fraud.

Hoffman and Brodley (1952) interviewed eighteen jurors after three trials in which objectionable testimony was introduced. Only one juror remembered that the evidence was not to be considered. Again, however, the number of cases investigated were too few to permit justifiable inferences. Likewise, the researchers were unable to demonstrate that consideration of the evidence had any influence on trial outcomes.

Broeder (1959) reports an experiment, conducted as part of the University of Chicago Jury Project, in which thirty mock juries were exposed to one of three versions of an automobile liability case. When the defendant disclosed that he had no liability insurance, the average award among jurors was $33,000; when he disclosed that he had liability insurance, the average award increased to $37,000; and when the jury was told to disregard the information that he had liability insurance, the average award increased to $46,000. Although no statistical analysis of these data is provided, the observed differences seem large enough to warrant an assumption of possible significance. The fascinating aspect of this study is, of course, its findings that the objection and subsequent instructions to disregard the objectionable testimony appear to have *increased* the testimony's impact.

Kline and Jess (1966) exposed four juries to prejudicial pretrial publicity. During deliberation, the evidence was mentioned in all four juries. In three of the juries the person mentioning the information was reminded of the judge's instruction to disregard the information, and it was not mentioned again. In the fourth jury the information was actively used in reaching a verdict. Again, the small number of juries mandates cautious interpretation.

Simon (1966) reports that when explicitly told to disregard prejudicial information obtained from sensational newspaper accounts, jurors who read such accounts return no more guilty verdicts than do jurors who read less sensational accounts. Sue et al. (1973) note, however, that the evidence introduced was not clearly important to the trial, and since it was from a newspaper, it might be easier to disregard than evidence heard during the trial itself.

Mitchell and Byrne (1973) detected no differences in verdicts between persons reading a transcript in which the judge instructed them to pay special attention to certain information and one in which he directed them to disregard it. They conclude that the instructions had no effect. In a similar vein, Sue et al. (1973) had students read one-page summaries of a trial in which a single instance of objectionable testimony was introduced. An objection to this evidence was either sustained or overruled and a control condition containing no objectionable evidence was also included. The researchers found that if the other information against the defendant was weak, the objectionable evidence resulted in significantly more convictions regardless of the judge's instructions. Both of these studies involved subjects reading brief transcripts or summaries of trials, and the extent to which one can generalize from such research to actual courtroom situations is open to question.

If jurors are influenced by inadmissible material, just what form does this influence take? Some rather involved hypothesizing, based on both legal wisdom and behavioral research, is possible with regard to this issue. The intended beneficiary of instances of improper questioning or of inadmissible testimony may indeed enjoy some increment of favorability for his or her case. This possibility, it seems, has encouraged some attorneys to introduce to the jury information they are aware is inadmissible. In moderation, this technique may work to the advantage of the attorney's case. However, when large numbers of instances of inadmissible material are inserted into a trial, their total effect might be quite different. Since trial procedure can be thought of as highly rule-governed, jurors can be assumed to have expectations paralleling these rules, i.e., jurors would expect that attorneys would not violate courtroom rules. If these rules are extensively violated by an attorney, then one or both of two contingencies might be predicted. The rule-breaking attorney might be perceived by jurors as having knowingly and intentionally broken the rules, in which case the attorney would be perceived as less trustworthy than had he or she not broken the rules. Alternatively, the rule-breaking attorney might be perceived as ignorant of the rules of trial procedure, leading to a decrement in the jurors' perceptions of his or her legal competence or expertise.

Whether an attorney's trustworthiness or competence is adversely affected by rule-breaking, it may be hypothesized that the decrement could well influence the client's case. Again, this effect could take one of two forms: in one case, jurors may react unfavorably toward the client represented by the rule-breaking attorney; in another, jurors may feel some measure of sympathy for the client and react more favorably toward the client's case.

## EFFECTS OF DELETING INADMISSIBLE MATERIAL ON PREDELIBERATION JUROR RESPONSES

Since the preceding analysis involves a number of complex,

competing, curvilinear relationships, no hypotheses were tested in our first study. Rather, the study was designed to address the following questions:

(1) Are there differences in verdicts among jurors exposed to differing amounts of inadmissible material in a civil trial?

(27 Among jurors finding for the plaintiff, are there differences in the amount of award among those jurors who have been exposed to differing amounts of inadmissible material?

(3) Are there differences in perceptions of attorney credibility among jurors who have been exposed to differing amounts of inadmissible material?

## Procedures

The automobile injury case (Nugent v. Clark) described in Chapter 3 was used in this study. In consultation with legal experts, we edited the trial dialogue to eliminate inadmissible material not actually contested in the original trial and to ensure an identical number of objections by both attorneys. As mentioned in Chapter 3, the edited transcript contained six objections by each of the attorneys, two of which were sustained by the judge and four of which were overruled. For each attorney, four of the objections concerned substantive matters — i.e., matters relating to the introduction of facts or opinions as evidence in the case — and two concerned procedural matters — i.e., matters relating to errors in trial procedure. This equalizing procedure made it possible to keep the merits of the two cases and the behavior of the two attorneys relatively comparable and to establish an identical baseline for the insertion of additional inadmissible material.

Originally, we contemplated varying numerous aspects of the introduction of inadmissible material: the number and ratio of such materials introduced by each of the attorneys, the number and ratio of objections sustained or overruled by the judge, etc. It quickly became obvious that if we wished to use the realistic setting of an actual courtroom and to use real jurors in the research, time constraints and financial resources prohibited such an ambitious scheme. Thus, we edited the original manuscript to allow us to study the possible impact of inadmissible material on a more modest scale.

Working with legal consultants, we constructed six additional instances of substantively objectionable material. These instances were all parts of the plaintiffs' case, i.e. they were either introduced by the content of questions asked by plaintiffs' attorney, or elicited from witnesses as a result of questioning by plaintiffs' attorney. The six instances of inadmissible material inserted in the trial were as follows:

(1) Plaintiffs' attorney questions the defendant, Frank Clark, about a prior arrest for drunken driving.

(2) Plaintiffs' attorney questions the defendant, Frank Clark, about his ownership of a motorcycle.

(3) Plaintiffs' attorney questions the defendant, Frank Clark, concerning alleged brake repairs on his auto following the accident.

(4) As a result of questioning by plaintiffs' attorney, the investigating officer testifies that there was damage on Frank Clark's car from a previous accident.

(5) As a result of questioning by plaintiffs' attorney, the attending physician expresses the opinion that Marjorie Nugent's life was probably shortened by the accident.

(6) As a result of questioning by her attorney, plaintiff Marjorie Nugent testifies that because of their excellent driving records, she and her husband have safe driver insurance rates.

Two criteria were used to prepare inadmissible materials: first, they should lend themselves to believable, "natural" insertions into the transcript; second, the psychological impact of each instance on the jurors should be roughly comparable. The first criterion was easier to satisfy than the second. At present, we know of no foolproof way to assure that each instance of inadmissible material will have an equal psychological impact on jurors. In making our choices, we were guided by the advice of legal consultants and by some pretesting of items on students and colleagues. Still, we seriously doubt that each instance is of equal psychological potency.

The six instances of inadmissible material were appropriately inserted into the original edited trial transcript, thus enabling us to create differing versions of the trial by editing out various numbers of them. The approach chosen focuses on measures of juror verdicts for the plaintiffs and on their perceptions of the plaintiffs's attorney. Therefore, any effects of the inadmissible material should be reflected by the frequency with which jurors find in favor of plaintiffs and their perceptions of the competence and trustworthiness of the plaintiffs' attorney.

One hundred and twenty jurors serving on the Wayne County Circuit Court (Detroit, Michigan), February 1974, panel, who voluntarily returned for "further jury service" during the week following the end of their term, were instructed that they would serve as jurors in change of venue trials moved to Wayne County from Michigan's upper peninsula. The jurors were randomly assigned to one of seven experimental conditions (zero deletions of inadmissible testimony to six deletions of inadmissible testimony). Each group was placed in rooms containing folding chairs and videotape equipment (one videotape recorder, one monitor per room).

The jurors were then shown the stimulus trial. Recesses at fifty-minute intervals and a lunch break were allowed. Visual exhibits were distributed at the appropriate time.

At the conclusion of the judge's instructions, which appeared on the videotape, all jurors completed the questionnaire containing the measuring instruments. After its completion, all jurors were completely debriefed. No juror expressed suspicion of the procedures used in the study.

The verdict measure was derived from the presiding judge's instructions to the jurors and followed closely from the substance of his remarks. Was, in fact, the defendant, Frank Clark, guilty of negligence in the case under consideration? If so, was the plaintiff, Marjorie Nugent, also guilty of contributory negligence? the measure consisted of a direct question about the jurors' evaluation of each of these questions. There were three possible responses: (1) defendant-Clark not negligent;

(2) defendant-Clark negligent, plaintiff-Nugent negligent; and
(3) defendant-Clark negligent, plaintiff-Nugent not negligent.

The award measure was also derived from the presiding judge's instructions to the jurors. If a juror found Clark guilty of negligence and Nugent not negligent (3 above), then he or she was required to specify the amount of money due Mr Nugent for the reimbursement of bills (derivative action) and the amount of money due Mrs Nugent for pain and suffering. Jurors were allowed to award Mr Nugent a maximum of $3,136 and Mrs Nugent a maximum of $42,500. Presented with these instructions and limitations, each juror responded by providing a judgment of an award for both Mr Nugent and Mrs Nugent, which could range from nothing to the maximum.

The measure of credibility for the plaintiffs' attorney consisted of a set of sixteen semantic differential scales that tap the competence and trustworthiness dimensions of credibility (Berlo et al., 1969-1970; McCroskey, 1966). The jurors noted the credibility of each attorney, even though we were primarily interested in their perceptions of the plaintiffs' attorney.

### TABLE 5.1
### Verdict Responses for Jurors in the Seven Conditions
### of Inadmissible Material

| Number of Deletions | Clark Neg | Both Clark Neg not Neg |
|---|---|---|
| 0 | 10 | 5 |
| 1 | 11 | 9 |
| 2 | 13 | 7 |
| 3 | 9 | 9 |
| 4 | 5 | 4 |
| 5 | 15 | 5 |
| 6 | 9 | 6 |

$X^2 = 3.25$; p $>$ .05

## Results

To test for effects of the deletion of inadmissible material on juror verdict, a chi-square test for differences in verdict among the seven conditions was performed. Table 5.1 indicates a generally higher proportion of verdicts for the plaintiff, but verdict does not vary significantly as the amount of inadmissible material introduced to jurors varies.

The mean awards made by jurors in the seven conditions are found in Table 5.2. To test for differences in the amount awarded to Marjorie Nugent, an analysis of variance in the amount of award given among the seven conditions was performed. Only the awards made by jurors who had found the defendant negligent and the plaintiff not negligent were considered in this analysis. That is, since no other jurors could legally have made awards, only those who found the defendant solely negligent were considered. The analysis yielded no significant differences attributable to the number of instances of inadmissible material included in the trial (F = < 1, p > .05).

To test for the effects of the inclusion of inadmissible material on the credibility of the plaintiffs' attorney, the sets of scales previously found to be highly reliable indicators of perceived trustworthiness and perceived competence were analyzed. Analysis of variance of both trustworthiness and competence scores did not produce any significant differences

### TABLE 5.2
**Mean Amount of Award by Jurors Viewing Trials with Varying Amounts of Inadmissible Material**

| Number of Deletions | Number of Awards | Number in Condition | Mean Award |
|---|---|---|---|
| 0 | 10 | 15 | $21,000 |
| 1 | 11 | 20 | 14,863 |
| 2 | 13 | 20 | 18,461 |
| 3 | 9 | 18 | 17,055 |
| 4 | 5 | 10 | 21,940 |
| 5 | 15 | 20 | 17,200 |
| 6 | 9 | 15 | 22,500 |

among the seven conditons of inadmissible material (F for trustworthiness = < 1, F for competence = 1.61, p > .05 in both instances).

## Discussion

This study discovered none of the effects of inadmissible material discussed previously. No statistically significant differences in verdict, amount of money awarded to plaintiff, or juror-perceived credibility of the offending attorney were observed. Several problems with the study may possibly explain this lack of differences. First, research that uses actual jurors sometimes poses unexpected procedural problems. For instance, the sample size of this study was approximately halved when, the day before we were to begin the research, several juries were drawn for actual trials. With such a small sample size, the likelihood of Type 2 error is high.

Second, examining the influence of inadmissible material on verdict, award, and attorney credibility by adding one to six instances to a four-hour trial may never have reached the point at which an attorney's rule-breaking behavior might work against him. Furthermore, the study may never have reached the point at which it begins to help the attorney and his client.

Therefore, the absence of differences for varying amounts of inadmissible material may be attributable to one or more of three things; (1) the inadmissible material may have had too small an effect in relation to the length of the trial; (2) the content of the instances of inadmissible material may have been neither supportive enough of plaintiffs' case, nor damning enough for defendant's case to appreciably influence the verdict, the award, or attorney credibility; or (3) the large amount of money asked for by the plaintiff, Mrs Nugent, may have suppressed any between-condition effects that may have existed. This suppression could have occurred because of the small sample size or because of the tendency of people to round off large numbers and to cluster them at the extremes of the allowable ends.

As indicated above, a pretest of the effect of the content of each item of inadmissible material was performed on a sample of students. The resulting rankings and ratings seemed comparable at the time. Nevertheless, because of the limited sample and the lack of opportunity to assess the impact of any instance of inadmissible testimony on a group of people in the context of the trial situation, we remained uncertain about whether the six instances of inadmissible materials were comparable in their impact on jurors.

## INADMISSIBLE MATERIAL AND PREDELIBERATION RESPONSES: A MODIFIED REPLICATION

A problem we have struggled with since the outset of this research concerns the question of *how much* and *what kind* of inadmissible materials are necessary if the judgments of jurors are to be influenced. Specifically, we have questioned whether or not the insertion of six additional items of inadmissible material is suffcient to sway the minds of jurors when they are viewing a trial that lasts almost four hours.

Perhaps, however, a problem may have arisen in our first study because of our attempt to detect very subtle differences. In that study, we depended on single-item differences in inadmissible materials to produce variations in juror response — i.e., our use of seven conditions relied heavily on the possibility that one additional item, or one less item, would exercise a powerful impact on juror behavior. Given that we had no precise way of gauging the psychological impact of each item, this procedure involved definite risks.

In our modified replication, we sought to discover if more extreme discriminations would exert differing effects on juror response. We used three of the seven conditions employed in our first study: the version of the trial containing none of the six additional items of inadmissible material, the version containing three of these items, and the version containing all six. The questions investigated paralleled those of the first study:

(1) Are there differences in attribution of negligence among jurors exposed to differing amounts of inadmissible material in a civil trial?

(27 Among jurors finding for the plaintiff, are there differences in the amount of award among those jurors who have been exposed to differing amounts of inadmissible material?

(3) Are there differences in perceptions of attorney credibility among jurors who have been exposed to differing amounts of inadmissible material?

## Procedures

Because of limitations in the availability of a courtroom setting and actual impaneled jurors, 144 undergraduate students at Michigan State University role-played jurors in this study. Potential jurors responded to advertisements requesting paid assistance in a legal research project, and those who agreed to participate were randomly assigned to one of the three conditions.

The study was conducted over a period of three evenings, with the same large classroom used each time. One of the conditions was run each evening. Three television monitors were used in each condition.

Role-playing jurors were told that they would be viewing an actual videotaped trial and that they were to behave like conscientious jurors. They were instructed to assume that their verdict would be binding on the plaintiff and the defendant.

After ascertaining that the jurors understood the instructions, the researcher started the recorder and played the appropriate version of the trial. Jurors were given a ten-minute break every hour while the researcher changed tapes. They were admonished not to talk about the trial during the breaks.

Following presentation of the entire trial, the role-playing jurors completed the same questionnaire used in the previous study. They were then debriefed by the researcher, thanked for their participation, and excused. Most of the jurors expressed interest in the project, and it appeared that they went about their task of role-playing jurors conscientiously.

## Results

Once again, there is no indication that the amount of inadmissible material affects jurors' verdicts. Table 5.3 summarizes the frequency of each type of verdict for role-playing jurors in the 0-item, 3-item, and 6-item conditions. The obtained chi-square does not approach significance. In this instance, more jurors found for the defendant, but the relative frequency is not affected by the various versions of the trial.

Moreover, there is no compelling evidence that the amount of inadmissible material introduced in the trial influenced the awards of jurors finding in favor of the plaintiff. The mean award for Mrs Nugent in the 0-item condition was $15,528; in the 3-item condition, $17,806; and in the 6-item condition, $14,964. Although this pattern of means is consistent with our expectations — i.e., when compared with the baseline version containing no additional inadmissible materials, Mrs Nugent's award went up with the addition of three items but declined with the further addition of three more — the analysis of variance does not approach significance ($F = <1$, $p > .05$).

Finally, there is no indication that jurors in the three conditions perceived the plaintiffs' attorney as differentially credible, suggesting that his introduction of inadmissible material did not have a deleterious effect on his courtroom image. Although the mean credibility ratings correspond with the pattern observed for amount of award — i.e., the plaintiffs' attorney's credibility

### TABLE 5.3
### Verdict Responses for Jurors in the Three Conditions
### of Inadmissible Material

| Number of Deletions | Clark Neg | Both Neg | Clark not Neg |
|---------------------|-----------|----------|---------------|
| 0 | 15 | | 26 |
| 3 | 20 | | 30 |
| 6 | 24 | | 29 |

$X^2 = 3.03$, $p > .05$

increased when he introduced three items of inadmissible testimony but declined when he increased the input to six items — the analysis of these ratings is not significant ($F = 1.70$, $p > .05$).

## Discussion

Overall, the results of two rather extensive studies suggest that the presence or absence of inadmissible material exerts a minimal impact on juror response. To be sure, our data reflect some weak trends for certain measures — e.g., there is some indication that jury verdicts and attorney credibility are curvilinearly related to the amount of inadmissible material introduced — but, in general, the influence of inadmissible material, as we defined and introduced it in these studies, on juror verdicts, awards, and perceptions of attorney credibility is minimal.

We earlier speculated on some possible procedural reasons for these findings. We lean toward the belief, however, that the results accurately represent the outcomes of the trial process. Stated differently, the presence of typical mundane instances of inadmissible material may have little effect on juror decisions; they may indeed be able to heed the judge's admonition to disregard this material. Although such a conclusion is not nearly as earth-shaking as a dramatic demonstration that an instance or two of inadmissible material exerted a powerful impact on the judgments of jurors, its implications for the everyday conduct of trials may be more significant. After all, few would question that an extremely startling or damaging instance of inadmissible material will have a noticeable influence on jurors. Had we chosen to use such material, we are confident that more extreme differences in juror response could have been generated. But such material constitutes the exception rather than the rule, and we were more interested in approximating the kind of deviations from normal procedure that appear in daily courtroom trials than we were in creating a spectacular case of trial process violation.

It is possible, then, that the deletion capabilities of videotaping are primarily of value for the latter kind of cases. For the average, everyday rule violations that occur, it may be unnecessary to expunge them from the psyches of jury members. Jurors may be capable of reaching decisions without being seriously influenced by such material. Of course, these outcomes are limited to individual predeliberation responses of jurors, and do not reflect the possible influence of inadmissible material on actual jury deliberation. We turn next to a study which included an opportunity for jurors to deliberate and reach a common verdict.

## EFFECTS OF DELETING INADMISSIBLE MATERIAL ON JURY DELIBERATION AND VERDICT

This study sought to determine if inadmissible material is discussed during jury deliberation, as well as whether such material affects jury verdicts. Specifically, we addressed the following questions:

(1) Do jurors exposed to inadmissible material discuss it during deliberation even though instructed to disregard it?
(2) Are there differences in verdicts between juries exposed to a trial containing inadmissible material and juries viewing the same trial without the inadmissible material?
(3) Are there differences in verdicts between juries exposed to a trial containing inadmissible material who discuss it during deliberation and juries who are exposed to the material but do not discuss it?
(4) Are there differences in certainty of verdicts between jurors exposed to a trial containing inadmissible material and jurors viewing the same trial without the inadmissible material?
(5) Are there differences in satisfaction with verdict between jurors exposed to a trial containing inadmissible material and jurors viewing the same trial without the inadmissible material?

### Procedures

As in previous studies, we chose to use a transcript of an actual trial rather than creating a mock trial. The following criteria were employed to select a transcript appropriate for this study:

(1) The trial should be no longer than an hour and thirty minutes in length.
(2) The evidence in the trial should be balanced, i.e., the evidence should not be heavily weighted in favor of the plaintiff or the defendant.
(3) The trial should contain an average number of objections for a trial of this length or should have the potential of being altered such that the number of objections would equal the average.

The first criterion was invoked for pragmatic reasons. Since the study was to focus upon deliberation, a lengthy trial would have increased the amount of time required of jurors, increasing the difficulty of obtaining an adequate sample.

The second criterion was applied in an effort to minimize biasing effects that would contaminate the dependent measures. Specifically, if the evidence in the trial were heavily weighted in favor of either the plaintiff or the defendant, a suppressor effect might be introduced that would militate against observing any effects of inadmissible material.

The third criterion was employed to maximize the generalizability of the findings. This criterion was difficult to satisfy given the absence of normative data concerning the "average" number of objections that occur in trials. In an effort to generate some normative guidelines, albeit rough ones, a number of legal experts with extensive trial experience were interviewed. Their pooled estimates suggested that a typical civil trial would contain approximately six objections per hour of trial activity.

With the aid of legal experts and guided by these criteria, a trial was selected involving a civil case in which the defendant was accused of conversion of funds by a bank. The original transcript contained two instances of inadmissible testimony and approximately one hour of trial testimony. The evidence presented during the original trial was not weighted heavily in favor of either the plaintiff or the defendant. Consequently, the first and second criteria were satisfied but not the third. Given that the testimony in the trial was approximately one hour in length, four additional instances of inadmissible evidence, each approximately one minute long, were constructed and inserted into the trial manuscript. In addition, the original instances of inadmissible evidence were rewritten to make them approximately one minute in length.

The transcript was edited to the extent that all references to the actual participants were deleted. The edited transcript was subsequently reviewed by the judge and two attorneys to ensure that the evidence in the trial was still balanced after the editing and the addition of the four instances of inadmissible testimony. The entire six items were as follows:

(1) The plaintiff's attorney summarizes in the absence of sufficient testimony a portion of evidence concerning the degree to which the plaintiff knows the defendant.
(2) In response to questioning by the plaintiff's attorney, the plaintiff offers hearsay evidence and states that the defendant is dishonest.
(3) The defense attorney contends that the plaintiff will lose her job if she cannot identify the individual who took the money from the bank.
(4) The plaintiff's attorney objects to the defense attorney's line of questioning of a witness and accuses him of badgering the witness.
(5) The plaintiff's attorney objects to a portion of evidence being entered as a matter of record without corroborating evidence.
(6) The plaintiff's attorney asks the defendant to speculate about who made the transaction at the bank.

Professional actors were recruited to play the roles of the plaintiff, defendant, witnesses, and the two attorneys. The judge who originally heard the case played himself in the trial reenactment. The trial was reenacted in an actual courtroom and videotaped in color using a single camera, and in black-and-white using a multicamera system. (This system will be discussed in detail in Chapter 6, when we report results of the multicamera versus single-camera production study.) A copy of the color videotape was made and electronically edited using a clean edit to remove the inadmissible material.

The full-screen color videotape was used as the stimulus for the study. Two different conditions were included, a treatment group in which participants viewed the version of the trial containing all six instances of inadmissible material and a control group in which participants viewed the version of the trial containing zero instances of inadmissible material.

Due to the lack of courtroom facilities and the need to unobtrusively videotape deliberations, the study was executed in a conference room in the Department of Communication at Michigan State University. The room was equipped with video recording cameras which were hidden in audio speaker boxes mounted on the walls.

One hundred and eighty adults from the Lansing area eligible for jury duty were recruited to role-play jurors in this study and were assigned to thirty, six-person juries. Fifteen juries were assigned to the control group and fifteen to the treatment group. Even though participants were notified well in advance, a few participants contacted us on the day they had agreed to participate and indicated they would be unable to keep their commitment. These last minute cancellations necessitated the use of confederates to maintain an atmosphere of realism for the remaining five jurors who expected to serve on a six-person jury. The actual role-playing jurors were unaware that the confederates were not participants like themselves, and the confederates were trained to maintain a low profile during the deliberations so they would not influence discussions among jurors nor their verdict votes.

On the evening of their participation, the role-playing jurors reported to the conference room and completed a questionnaire focusing on demographic information. These data were used to ensure that the jurors assigned to both the treatment and control groups were comparable. The jurors then viewed the trial.

After viewing the trial and prior to beginning deliberations, the jurors elected a foreperson who polled the jury via written ballot to determine their predeliberation verdicts. The confederates voted "undecided" during this initial polling and when the foreperson announced the result of this vote, the confederates voted with the majority during subsequent pollings until a verdict was reached. These activities and the deliberation proceedings were recorded on videotape.

Once a verdict had been reached and reported to the experimenter in charge, the jurors completed a second questionnaire containing measures of satisfaction with verdict and certainty of verdict. After this questionnaire was completed, the role-playing jurors were informed they had been videotaped and were given the opportunity to have the tape erased. The reasons for the unobtrusive videotaping procedure were carefully explained to them including the possibility that they might have behaved in a different manner had they been aware of the videotaping process. None of the jurors objected to the videotaping and agreed with the necessity for the unobtrusive procedures employed. Moreover, most of them were quite enthusiastic about the research and spent considerable time reviewing the videotape record of their deliberation proceedings.

## Results

Jurors exposed to inadmissible material sometimes discussed the inadmissible evidence; in fact, eight of the fifteen juries exposed to testimony ruled inadmissible discussed it during their deliberation proceedings. Although no statistical test could be performed on the verdicts because of small cell frequencies for guilty verdicts, it is quite apparent that jurors exposed to inadmissible material, whether it was discussed or not, did not report verdicts significantly different from their counterparts who were not exposed to it (Table 5.4). Almost all of the juries in the control and inadmissible conditions found the defendant innocent while only one jury in either condition found him guilty.

Even though no significant differences were observed for the certainty of verdict measure, the results approached significance ($t$ = 1.85, p <.10, two-tailed). Specifically, jurors who heard the inadmissible material were more confident that their verdicts were correct (M = 4.68) than their counterparts not exposed to the inadmissible material (M = 4.29).

Finally, there was no significant difference in satisfaction with verdict between jurors exposed to inadmissible material and those who were not exposed to it ($t$ = 1.04, p >.05, two-tailed).

## Discussion

Two important findings emerged from this study. First, juries exposed to inadmissible material may discuss it even though instructed to disregard it. Second, while jurors exposed to inadmissible material tend to be more certain of the correctness of their verdicts than jurors not exposed to it, the verdicts arrived at are essentially the same.

The finding that exposure to, and even discussion of inadmissible material does not appear to influence verdict outcomes even though it influences certainty of verdict is subject to one note of caution. Although care was taken to ensure that a trial

**TABLE 5.4**
**Jury Verdicts for Inadmissible Material and Control Conditions**

|          | Inadmissible Condition | Control Condition |
|----------|:----------------------:|:-----------------:|
| Innocent | 12                     | 13                |
| Guilty   | 1                      | 1                 |
| Hung     | 2                      | 1                 |
| N        | 15                     | 15                |

transcript was selected in which the evidence relevant to both the plaintiff's and defendant's cases was balanced, the number of innocent verdicts favoring the defendant indicates that the search was not successful. The justification for this concern is reinforced by the relatively high level of certainty about correctness of verdict expressed by all the jurors regardless of the condition to which they were assigned. Of course, it is possible that when compared with the plaintiff, the defendant was a more convincing witness. Had the trial proved to be more balanced, the inadmissible material may have influenced not only certainty of verdicts but verdicts as well.

Taken together, the several studies we have conducted suggest that the impact of typical instances of inadmissible material may not be as marked as some social scientists and legal experts have contended. In no case did the presence or absence of inadmissible material exert a significant impact on juror verdicts or their perceptions of the rule-violating attorney. Although jurors frequently mentioned inadmissible material during deliberation, there was no indication that the introduction of the testimony affected the eventual verdict. Moreover, when inadmissible material was introduced into the deliberation by one of the jurors, other jurors frequently reminded the panel that the material should not influence the jury's verdict.

Naturally, our conclusions about inadmissible material must be treated cautiously. As previously noted, we attempted to use reasonably typical, somewhat mundane instances of objectionable testimony. Undoubtedly, some kinds of inadmissible material — for instance, dramatic, damning items of the type often seen in courtroom television dramas — are capable of influencing juror decision-making. Because of this fact and because jurors sometimes discuss inadmissible material during deliberation, expunging of inadmissible material still strikes us as a wise course of judicial action. The question remains as to the best method of accomplishing such editing, and we next consider a study dealing with this issue.

## JUROR RESPONSE TO VARIOUS METHODS
## OF EDITING INADMISSIBLE MATERIAL

Currently, there are four different methods that can be used to edit videotaped trial materials: (1) the *clean* edit, (2) the *video only* edit, (3) the *blackout normal machine speed* edit, and (4) the *blackout fast forward* edit. Only the last three techniques are presently being used in the courtroom, because of time and cost considerations associated with the clean edit.

### Clean Edit Method

Clean editing actually removes the objectionable material from the videotape. The original tape is copied onto another tape, but the inadmissible material is left out. The equipment used to copy the original tape has the capacity to edit videotape electronically. Thus, at the appropriate time for editing, the recorder is switched into the "edit" mode. At the end of the inadmissible testimony, the recorder is switched back into the "record" mode. This produces an uninterrupted tape, save for a possible momentary flick (i.e., a break in the visual pattern) in the video portion of the tape. However, this slight break in the visual pattern can be rendered virtually undetectable if the editing is done professionally.

### Video Only Method

The video only method entails removal of the audio portion of the tape. The operator sits in the courtroom and views the trial or the deposition on a small monitor while the jury simultaneously views the playback on larger monitors. The operator has the list of portions of the tape that are to be edited based on the judge's rulings. The time and date have previously been recorded on the tape by use of a time-date generator, and while this information is not visually displayed for the jurors on the large monitors, it is visually displayed on the operator's small monitor through a simple adjustment of the horizontal hold mechanism. At the exact second the edit is to begin, the operator electronically suppresses the audio signal from the tape without affecting the video signal. Consequently, the jury can see the visual information presented on the tape but does not hear any of the verbal exchanges. At the conclusion of the inadmissible material, the operator reactivates the audio signal. This procedure is repeated for each instance of inadmissible material appearing on the videotape.

### Blackout Normal Machine Speed Method

The procedure for the blackout normal machine speed method is the same as the procedure for the video only method save for one exception. The operator electronically suppresses both the audio and video signals on the tape. Thus, the jury neither hears nor sees the inadmissible material. What they see is a black screen, much the same as if the monitors had been turned off. However, even though the audio and video signals have been suppressed on the jurors' monitors, the video signal appears on the small monitor being used by the operator. By observing the time and date information on the videotape, the operator can reactivate the audio and video signals when the inadmissible material is over.

### Blackout Fast Forward Method

This method is the same as the previous one except for one difference. Besides electronically suppressing the video and audio signals, the operator advances the videotape at a faster speed for lengthy portions of inadmissible material. The decision concerning when the tape should be fast forwarded is somewhat arbitrary; however, segments that approach thirty seconds or longer in duration are usually fast forwarded.

### Problems Associated with These Methods

All four editing methods may be distracting to the jurors. Distraction has been defined as the occurrence of "absorbing sensory stimulation" that is irrelevant to the primary message being presented (Baron et al., 1973). Thus, for a stimulus to be distracting, it must be noticed by the person and the information conveyed by the stimulus must be unrelated to the primary message. Furthermore, information is defined as any stimulus an individual processes. Therefore, noise and silence can also be considered information cues which function as distracting stimuli.

The purpose of editing videotape trials or depositions is to remove irrelevant and biasing material. Ideally, the edit would occur in such a manner that the trial would flow continuously and the edit would not be detected by the jurors. Save for the possibility of the clean edit, the methods discussed above fail to achieve this ideal. Additionally, although the edits remove unwanted information, they themselves convey information. At a minimum, they indicate that something has been deleted from the videotape. Given the objective of editing, this information is superfluous to the primary content of the trial. Consequently, the edits themselves may distract the jurors.

Even the clean edit may produce a momentary break in the visual pattern. Although the actual edit lasts only a split-second, the visual image appearing on the monitors just before the edit may be quite different from the image immediately following it. The amount of difference depends, of course, upon how much movement among the trial participants occurred during the edited segment. Possibly the facial expressions of trial participants will differ or their physical positions in the courtroom may change. Any sudden shift in visual orientation — i.e., "unnatural" appearing movements of participants — may be distracting to jurors.

The video only method introduces additional distracting elements. Since the audio signal is suppressed without affecting the video signal, jurors are able to see the trial participants' movements but are unable to hear anything. The sudden loss of audio information, with the retention of visual information, constitutes an "unnatural" occurrence. An additional problem concerning the interpretation of nonverbal behaviors will be discussed in more detail later.

The two blackout methods eliminate the problem emanating from the presentation of visual stimuli when using the video only method. Nevertheless, use of either method disrupts the continuity of the trial. Jurors lose both visual and audio information. This loss constitutes information, albeit superfluous information.

When using either blackout method, the length of the edit must also be considered. Obviously, if the same material were edited using both methods, the duration of the edit would be shorter for the blackout fast forward method than for the blackout normal machine speed edit. One factor that influences the distraction potential of a stimulus is the length of time the receiver is exposed to it (Baron et al, 1973). Perhaps distracting stimuli lasting for short time periods have no significant effect upon jurors. Although we would expect the blackout fast forward method to be less distracting than the blackout normal machine speed method, no data presently exist to confirm our expectation. Additionally, knowledge concerning *how* distracting stimuli affect juror information-processing and decision-making activities would be useful when considering what editing method to use.

While not directly applicable, research on distraction and persuasion suggests some potential effects that distraction resulting from editing procedures may have upon jurors. Unfortunately, previous research focusing on distraction has produced seemingly inconsistent results. For example, distraction has been found both to increase the persuasibility of a message (Festinger and Maccoby, 1964; Rosenblatt, 1966; Shamo and Meador, 1969) and to decrease it (Gardner, 1966; Miller and Levy, 1967; Vohs and Garrett, 1968), to enhance the credibility of a speaker (Freedman and Sears, 1965) and to decrease it (Miller and Levy, 1967), and to increase recall of message content (Silverman and Regula, 1968) and to decrease it (Vohs, 1964; Gardner, 1966; Haaland and Venkatesan, 1968).

Although the preceding studies report inconsistent findings, there is a plausible explanation for the discrepancy. Baron et al. (1973) report that the effects of distraction are mediated by a number of factors including the perceived credibility of a source prior to the distraction and whether or not the distracting stimuli can be ignored. The first factor may account for the discrepant findings in those studies involving credibility, while the second may explain discrepancies concerning the persuasive impact of a message and the recall of message content (Baron et al., 1973).

There are important differences between the research on distraction and our concern about the distracting potential of various editing methods. In most distraction studies, the source of distraction has been something other than a message itself. When editing videotape, the distraction occurs in the message proper. Furthermore, in previous studies there has been only one message source, while in a videotaped trial, there are numerous sources. Given these differences, coupled with the numerous factors that influence distraction, predicting the effects of these editing methods on jurors is problematic.

Besides distraction, the two remaining editing methods pose other problems. Use of the clean edit introduces a cost problem. As mentioned earlier, this technique involves a special machine to edit videotape electronically. Presently, the cost of electronic editors, as well as technicians to operate them, is substantial. Furthermore, the time required to edit is much greater than for the other three methods.

In addition, the clean edit is the only method that actually *removes* inadmissible material from the tape. Granted, the original copy remains intact, but it would not be shown to the jury. This procedure creates concern about doctoring the tape. With proper care, edits can be rendered virtually undetectable; in fact, computerized editors are currently available that edit out professionally so that the edits would not be detectable. One solution to the removal problem would be to have the editing done in the presence of both attorneys and the judge. The tape would then be locked up until the jury was to view the trial.

The final method to be considered is the video only edit. As mentioned earlier, this editing procedure involves electronic suppression of the audio signal from the tape. Thus, only verbal information is denied to jurors. Ekman and Friesen (1974) found that people can detect deceptive communication from the nonverbal behavior of another person. Clearly, nonverbal information is still being presented to jurors when the video portion is shown, though it is difficult to predict how jurors might use this information. Much would depend on the nature of the trial, the events transpiring up to the point of the edit, who was on camera during the edit, and what they were doing.

Although the four methods of editing may have differing effects on jurors, a strong theoretical base for predictions does not exist. Consequently, this study was question-centered, rather than hypothesis-centered. Specifically, the following questions were examined:

(1) Do jurors exposed to different editing methods demonstrate differences in retention of trial-related information?
(2) Do jurors exposed to different editing methods demonstrate differences in their assessment of attorney credibility?
(3) Do jurors exposed to different editing methods report differing levels of distraction?
(4) Do jurors exposed to different editing methods report different verdicts?

## Procedures

The full-screen color videotape of the bank funds conversion case was used as a stimulus. Five versions of the trial were employed. In the *no edit* version, none of the inadmissible material was deleted. A second version was created by electronically editing out the inadmissible material using the clean edit procedure. The remaining three versions of the trial entailed the deletion of inadmissible material using the video only, the blackout normal machine speed, and the blackout fast forward methods respectively. These edits were executed during three different presentations of the trial to three different groups of jurors.

To ensure maximum generalizability of the findings, actual jurors viewed the videotapes in a real courtroom and received instructions from an actual judge. Judge Bruce Fox, 66th District Court of Shiawassee County, Corunna, Michigan, assisted with the study. Two hundred and twenty-five jurors drawn from the active jury list in Shiawassee County were randomly assigned to one of the five conditions and were summoned by the court to report for jury duty on one of five days, forty-five jurors for each day. As was expected, some jurors requested to be excused from jury duty, causing conditions to range in size from twenty-four to thirty-six jurors.

All of the jurors in each condition viewed the trial at the same time. The presiding judge introduced the trial, using the same jury size cover story employed in prior studies and assuring the jurors their verdict would be binding on the litigants. The judge went on to explain that the trial was to be presented by videotape, that it had been taped before a judge in Lansing, and that it was being shown in Corunna due to a large jury-case backlog in Lansing. The judge's instructions were the same for all five conditions save for slight changes to accommodate the particular editing method used on a given day.

After instructing the jurors, the judge left the courtroom to conduct other court business while the jurors watched the videotaped trial. The video technician operating the video equipment and the court clerk, Howard Hanchett, remained in the courtroom while the jurors watched the trial. Two videotape monitors were used for the playback to ensure that everyone could see and hear the trial.

At the conclusion of the trial, the judge returned to the courtroom and instructed the jurors regarding their pending deliberations and the law that was applicable to this case. The judge then asked the jurors to complete a questionnaire for the jury size study. Their responses to this questionnaire were used to answer the research questions.

## Measurement Techniques

This study focused upon the effects of various editing techniques upon the amount of information retained by jurors, juror perceptions of the credibility of trial participants, the level of distraction experienced by jurors, and the verdicts arrived at by jurors.

Amount of information retained by jurors was measured by a twenty-seven-item multiple choice test. Items were pretested using thirty-four undergraduate students enrolled in communication courses at Michigan State University. The students were shown the videotaped trial in which no editing methods were used. They then responded to forty-six information retention items, and items which exhibited low reliability or a low index of discrimination were culled.

Juror perceptions of the credibility of attorneys were again measured by semantic differential-type scales shown to load highly on the dimensions of trustworthiness, competence, and dynamism (Berlo et al., 1969-1970; McCroskey, 1966).

Distraction was indexed with a seven-interval scale bounded by the responses "extremely distracting" and "not at all distracting." Jurors assigned to the four conditions in which edits appeared were asked to rate the level of distraction of the editing method, while jurors in the no edit condition were asked to rate the level of distraction resulting from the objections raised by the attorneys. Finally, verdict was measured by having jurors indicate whether the defendant was guilty or innocent.

## Results

The mean retention scores for jurors in the various editing conditions are found in Table 5.5. Analysis of variance revealed

**TABLE 5.5**
**Mean Retention Scores for Jurors in the Five Conditions**

| No Edit | Clean Edit | Blackout Fast Forward | Blackout Normal Machine Speed | Video Only |
|---------|-----------|----------------------|-------------------------------|-----------|
| 18.75 | 17.84 | 19.10 | 19.17 | 19.89 |

that there were no significant differences in the amount of trial-related information retained by jurors exposed to the four types of editing methods ($F = < 1$, $p > .05$).

The mean credibility ratings for both the plaintiff's and defendant's attorneys are summarized in Table 5.6. Analysis of variance of the credibility ratings for the plaintifff's attorney yielded a significant F of 5.51 ($p < .05$). Subsequent condition by condition comparisons, using Dunnett's test (Edwards, 1960) for comparison of the no edit control group with each of the four editing conditions and the Newman-Keuls procedure (Winer, 1971) for comparing each of the four editing conditions, revealed that the plaintiff's attorney was perceived as significantly more credible in the no edit condition than in any of the four conditions where inadmissible material was edited. None of the four editing conditions differed significantly from each other.

These differences did not hold for credibility ratings of the defendant's attorney. The analysis of variance for these ratings revealed no significant differences among the five conditions ($F = < 1$, $p > .05$).

Mean distraction scores for jurors in each condition are found in Table 5.7. Analysis of variance of these scores indicated that perceived distraction was significantly affected by the type of editing method used ($F = 10.63$, $p < .05$). Comparisons of the no edit control condition with each of the editing conditions, using Dunnett's test, revealed that the clean edit was not significantly more distracting while each of the other three edits was significantly more distracting than no editing.

Results of the Newman-Keuls test indicated that the blackout fast forward condition did not differ significantly from the clean edit condition in the amount of distraction reported. However, the blackout normal machine speed and the video only conditions were perceived as being significantly more distracting than the clean edit condition. The blackout normal machine speed condition did not differ significantly from the blackout fast forward condition. The video only condition was perceived as being significantly more distracting than the

## TABLE 5.6
## Mean Credibility Ratings of Plaintiff and Defense Attorneys for Jurors in the Five Conditions*

|  | No Edit | Clean Edit | Blackout Fast Forward | Blackout Normal Machine Speed | Video Only |
|---|---|---|---|---|---|
| Plaintiff attorney | $85.35_a$ | $75.04_b$ | $78.18_b$ | $71.14_b$ | $72.92_b$ |
| Defense attorney | $82.55_c$ | $75.00_c$ | $78.46_c$ | $75.86_c$ | $75.15_c$ |

* In each row, means with different subscripts differ significantly from each other.

## TABLE 5.7
## Mean Reported Distraction Levels for Jurors in the Five Conditions*

| No Edit | Clean Edit | Blackout Fast Forward | Blackout Normal Machine Speed | Video Only |
|---|---|---|---|---|
| $2.38_a$ | $3.33_{ab}$ | $3.82_{bc}$ | $4.91_{cd}$ | $5.30_d$ |

* Means with a common letter do not differ significantly.

## TABLE 5.8
## Frequency of Verdicts for Jurors in the Five Conditions

|  | No Edit | Clean Edit | Blackout Fast Forward | Blackout Normal Machine Speed | Video Only |
|---|---|---|---|---|---|
| Guilty | 10 | 9 | 7 | 7 | 14 |
| Innocent | 23 | 16 | 19 | 16 | 13 |

blackout fast forward condition. No significant differences were found between the blackout normal machine speed condition and the video only condition. Thus, when the conditions are ordered from least distracting to most distracting, any two adjacent conditions were not found to be significantly different from each other. All other possible comparisons were found to be significantly different.

The verdicts reported by jurors in each condition are shown in Table 5.8. Results of a chi-square test indicated no significant differences in the verdict rendered by jurors in the five conditions $x^2 = 4.65$, $p > .05$).

Secondary correlation analyses revealed that distraction is significantly related to the credibility ratings of both attorneys; such that as distraction increases, perceived credibility decreases. Somewhat surprisingly, however, verdict did not correlate significantly with juror perceptions of either attorney's credibility or with the amount of trial-related information retained by jurors, though the tests are not highly sensitive due to the nominal scaling of the verdict measure.

## Discussion

Findings of this study clearly indicate a relationship between the various editing methods and the perceived credibility of the plaintiff's attorney. Since the relationship is such that the credibility of the plaintiff's attorney decreases in the edited conditions, it seems that the mere act of editing affects juror perceptions of credibility, at least for the plaintiff's attorney.

One possible explanation of this finding emanates from the expectations jurors may have concerning trials in general. The only procedural difference between the edited conditions and the no edit condition is the deletion of the objections and subsequent arguments between the two attorneys concerning the objections. Perhaps jurors expect to hear the objections raised by attorneys and to be privy to their arguments surrounding these objections. This information may itself be used by jurors to evaluate the expertise and competence of the attorneys.

By deleting the objections and the arguments germane to them, jurors may be denied information concerning the communication skills of the contesting attorneys, information that, in turn, affects their perceptions of the credibility of the attorneys. While jurors are instructed by the judge to disregard inadmissible material, no legal mandate requires them to disregard attorney behavior during the assessment of the admissibility or inadmissibility of trial material. Conceivably, then, a client's case could be seriously jeopardized by the incompetence of his or her attorney in spite of favorable trial testimony or evidence presented during the trial.

Jurors are undoubtedly naive about some procedures followed during a trial and about some aspects of the law applicable in any given case. Nevertheless, given the popularity of courtroom television dramas, it would be equally naive to assume that jurors have no expectations concerning courtroom trials and attorney behavior. Also, jurors possess common sense and intellect that not only aid in assessing the legal strategy used by attorneys during the course of a trial, but also enable them to furmulate the legal strategy they themselves would have used if they were acting as a trial attorney. In one sense, this is similar to the hindsight of the "Monday morning quarterback" who itemizes the shortcomings of a football coach's strategy during Sunday's game.

If jurors conclude that the attorney represented a client inadequately, they may disassociate the attorney from the client and base their verdict solely upon the testimonial information. If juror perceptions of either attorney's credibility were not extremely favorable and if they disassociate their decision-making from the attorneys' performance, we would not always expect to find a relationship between jurors' perceptions of attorney credibility and subsequent verdicts.

Granted, there are a number of important ifs in this explanation, and while we have no data bearing directly on this interpretation, those we do have indirectly support it. There was no significant relationship between juror perceptions of the credibility of the attorneys in this case and their verdicts. Moreover, the editing techniques affected only the perceived credibility of the plaintiff's attorney, and he was seen as slightly more credible than the defendant's attorney.

Additional anecdotal evidence supports this explanation. During their debriefings, jurors were quite vocal in their appraisals of the attorneys' performance. Most of them were not favorably impressed. They complained that both attorneys failed to ask important questions of witnesses. The jurors also felt that other individuals associated with the case should have testified during the trial; as a result, they believed the attorneys had presented an incomplete case. It is worth noting that many of the jurors compared this trial to courtroom television drama when evaluating the legal strategies used by the attorneys.

While jurors were critical of both attorneys, they were more dissatisfied with the defendant's attorney. Although the perceived credibility of the two attorneys did not differ significantly, the plaintiff's attorney was rated slightly higher. Furthermore, only the perceived credibility of the plaintiff's attorney was affected by the editing techniques. This suggests that the plaintiff's attorney's handling of issues regarding inadmissible material made a more favorable impression on jurors than the actions of the defendant's attorney.

A significant relationship was observed between the editing techniques and the amount of distraction experienced by the jurors. The differences were not uniform, nor were all of them statistically significant. The clean edit did not differ significantly from no editing, but the remaining editing methods were significantly more distracting than no editing. The blackout fast forward method did not differ significantly from the clean edit nor the blackout normal machine speed edit, but was significantly more distracting than no editing and significantly less distracting than the blackout normal machine speed method. Finally, the blackout normal machine speed method was not significantly different from the video only method.

One factor that could explain this pattern of relationships is the amount of time needed to execute the edits. Regardless of the material involved, the clean edit lasts for only a split-second. For the objectionable material used in this study, the blackout fast forward edit lasted an average of 17.33 seconds, while the blackout normal machine speed edit and the video only edit both lasted an average of 74.5 seconds. Clearly, the distraction effect of an edit that lasts for a split-second comes closer to approximating the no edit condition than any other condition. Our results indicate that an edit which lasts approximately 17 seconds is no more distracting than an edit that lasts for a split-second. Furthermore, the distraction of an edit which lasts for approximately 17 seconds is no greater than of an edit that lasts for approximately 74.5 seconds. This last comparison, however, is not entirely accurate. As noted above, both the blackout normal machine speed edit and the video only edit last an average of 74.5 seconds. Yet, the blackout fast forward edit is less distracting than the video only edit but not less distracting than the blackout normal machine speed edit. This may be due to the fact that the two blackout edits are identical except for the amount of time necessary to execute the edit. On the other hand, the video only edit differs from the blackout fast forward edit in the amount of information deleted as well as the amount of time necessary to execute the edit.

Apparently, differences in the amount of information deleted coupled with differences in time are necessary to produce a significant distraction difference when the edits range from seventeen seconds to seventy-four seconds. This possibility would account for the difference between the blackout fast forward edit and the video only edit. In addition, it would explain the lack of significant differences between the blackout normal machine speed edit and the video only edit. These last two edits differ in the amount of information deleted, but do not differ in the amount of time necessary to execute the edit. In short, there appears to be some critical level of time difference, such that if two editing techniques exceed that limit, then significant differences occur in the amount of distraction. If the limit is not exceeded, then significant differences will not occur, unless there is a discrepancy in the amount of information deleted. Precisely what difference in time constitutes a critical level is not clear from these results.

Distraction was found to be negatively related to the credibility of the plaintiff's attorney, and the relationship between this variable and the credibility of the defendant's attorney was also negative, though not significantly so. Since past research on persuasion has shown that distraction increases the persuasibility of a message and since high credible communicators are more persuasive than low credible sources, it may initially seem that distraction and credibility should be positively related.

One possible explanation for the negative relationship between distraction and credibility lies in the characteristics of the setting of this study and the sample employed. In most distraction research, the sample used consisted of college undergraduates. Furthermore, participants in these studies were usually presented a message from one source and changes in attitude toward the topic and/or the source were measured. However, the context of the present study is quite different. Actual jurors were asked to evaluate messages from more than one source and to reach a decision that would have important consequences for the litigants. In other words, the demands of an actual trial are very different from those of a classroom setting where people are asked to listen to one persuasive message. More research is needed to determine whether the findings from previous distraction research are generalizable to courtroom situations similar to the one employed in this study.

The findings from this study have definite implications for the legal community. First, the editing of inadmissible material appears to result in a decrease in perceived credibility of the trial participants. The problem lies in finding out why this effect occurs. If it occurs because editing of testimony violates juror expectations concerning what is supposed to happen in a trial, then a solution would be to restructure these expectations through judicial instructions.

A second major implication concerns the amount of distraction associated with each editing method. Given the negative relationship between distraction and credibility, the best method to use would be the one with the least amount of distraction associated with it. Based on the results of this study, the clean edit would be advised. However, if the objections were short enough, another edit might suffice. This possibility awaits further research aimed at establishing time levels more precisely.

Based on present findings, as well as our experience while executing the various editing methods, the following recommendations are offered. Of the four editing methods examined, the best method to use is the clean edit. The clean edit was not more distracting then the no edit condition, while the other techniques were all more distracting. Moreover, if a clean edit is executed skillfully, jurors are unaware that editing has occurred. We observed that when jurors knew material was edited, they speculated about its content, an activity that might be even more biasing than knowing what the excerpt contained and being instructed to disregard it.

If the costs of performing the clean edit are prohibitive, then another method could be used under certain conditions. If the material to be edited is less than seventeen seconds, then the blackout normal machine speed method appears satisfactory. The blackout fast forward method is not recommended due to the difficulty involved in executing the edit. The operator must attend closely to the trial, as well as the speed of the machine while advancing the tape. It is relatively easy for the operator to advance the tape too far, or not far enough, which increases the time needed to execute the edit. The added time may heighten distraction, which in turn may affect the perceived credibility of the attorneys. Finally, the video only method is not recommended under any circumstances. This method was perceived as the most distracting of all the edits. Furthermore, it does not eliminate all of the information that transpires during inadmissible portions of the trial. For these reasons, the video only technique is considered inferior to the other three methods.

## SUMMING UP

This chapter has described the results of four studies investigating juror response to the deletion of inadmissible material from videotaped trials and depositions. The outcomes of the first two studies, which dealt with the possible influence of inadmissible material on juror predeliberation verdicts and their perceptions of the rule-violating attorney, indicated that the presence or absence of such material exerted no significant impact on these two juror responses. We stressed that one reason for this lack of significance may lie in our use of typical, relatively mundane inadmissible material, rather than the kinds of dramatic, highly incriminating items used in much previous research.

We next reported the findings of a study that sought to determine whether jurors discuss inadmissible material during deliberation; and if so, whether such dialogue influences the subsequent jury verdict. Although jurors frequently discussed the inadmissible material, there was no indication that their exchanges significantly affected the jury's verdict.

Finally, we presented the results of a study in which four different editing methods were compared. Not surprisingly, we found that edits which are minimally obtrusive and time-consuming exert the least disruptive impact on jurors and should therefore be used whenever time and cost considerations permit.

*6*

# VIDEO PRODUCTION TECHNIQUES
# AND JUROR RESPONSES

Along with our interest in juror responses to alternative presentation modes and the effects of deleting inadmissible materials from video presentations, we were concerned with the potential influence of various video production techniques on juror responses. Three studies investigated the effects of various production techniques upon juror information-processing and decision-making behaviors.

## JUROR RESPONSES TO SPLIT-SCREEN
## AND FULL-SCREEN TRIALS

Full-screen videotaped presentations have the potential of reducing the amount of nonverbal information provided to jurors. The nonverbal behaviors exhibited by witnesses and attorneys might be more difficult to observe when a full-screen panoramic shot of the trial proceedings is used. More specifically, the facial affect displays would be difficult to see when video cameras are not tightly focused in on testifying witnesses. It is also conceivable, given this loss of information, that juror interest in videotaped proceedings may be adversely affected.

However, a camera shot which only presented the testifying witness and perhaps the interrogating attorney would also result in a loss of information for jurors. They would be denied access to the nonverbal responses of other trial participants sitting in the courtroom. For these reasons, a split-screen format was developed which included a closeup shot of the testifying witnesses and interrogating attorneys, as well as a panoramic view of the other trial participants in the courtroom. The effects on juror responses to this presentation format were compared to the effects of a full-screen presentation.

Although the differences between these two systems were discussed in Chapter 3, they will be briefly reviewed here. Perhaps the greatest difference in the two systems resides in the amount of detail that can be captured by the cameras. Although the single camera full-screen system has the advantage of providing jurors with a realistic shot of the entire trial area, the technical limitations of relatively low-cost equipment prevent the screening of closeup views of trial participants, particularly when panning and zooming are prohibited. Thus, while the full-screen shot enables jurors to identify the various participants, it does not permit them to pick up many subtle nuances in facial expression, gesture, and the like.

By contrast, the triple camera, split-screen system allows the juror to study the idiosyncratic responses of trial participants in greater detail. The two camera shots that comprise the upper half of the screen — the shot of the witness in the upper left quarter and of the questioning attorney and the bench in the upper right quarter — provide much more detailed shots of the participants because the cameras are focused tightly on those portions of the trial area. The greatest potential disadvantage of the split-screen system is its lack of realism; unlike the full-screen system, which communicates a single shot of a familiar setting, the split-screen system obviously relies upon technology to create a more highly visible, yet somehow more "unnatural" product.

How are these differences likely to affect juror responses, if at all? Again, we believed it possible to make plausible arguments for either, or several, opposing outcomes. On the one hand, the greater detail of the split-screen system might provide more information for jurors, thereby allowing them to make finer discriminations in their perceptions of trial participants or to assimilate more trial-related information. On the other hand, the contrived nature of the split-screen system might itself be distracting, causing jurors to become curious about the ways the production effect is achieved. To the extent that this might happen, we would expect assimilation of trial-related information to suffer.

Since we were uncertain which lines of argument might prove most fruitful, we decided, as in several of the other studies discussed, to pose questions rather than to test hypotheses:

(1) Are there differences in verdicts between jurors exposed to full-screen and split-screen trials?

(2) Among jurors finding for the plaintiff, are there differences in the amount of award between those who viewed the full-screen and those who viewed the split-screen trial?

(3) Are these differences in perceptions of attorney credibility between jurors exposed to full-screen and split-screen trials?

(4) Are there differences in retention of trial-related information between jurors exposed to full-screen and split-screen trials?

(5) Are there differences in motivation and interest between jurors exposed to full-screen and split-screen trials?

## Procedures

The automobile injury case (Nugent v. Clark) described in Chapter 3 was used in this study. Role-playing jurors were fifty-seven adult members of a Catholic church group in the greater Lansing area. Aside from the obvious bias in religious affiliation, the participants' demographic characteristics — e.g., age, occupation, and educational level — were similar to those of a typical jury panel. Constraints concerning the availability of a courtroom and of actual impaneled jurors led to our decision to conduct the study outside the courtroom setting.

Participants were randomly assigned to either the full-screen or the split-screen condition. They were told that they would be viewing a reenacted trial concerning an automobile injury case and that they were to assume the role of jurors. It was further explained that the purpose of the study was to assess both the effects of using videotape in courtroom trials and the effects of jury size on the responses of individual jurors. The importance of entering into the role of juror was stressed, and it appeared that most of the participants assumed the role earnestly.

After the instructions had been given, jurors in the full-screen condition saw the single-camera videotape while jurors in the split-screen condition saw the triple-camera tape of the same trial. The trial was shown in fifty-minute segments, with the jurors taking a ten-minute break between each segment while the researcher put the next reel on the machine. The jurors were cautioned not to discuss the trial during the breaks. When the trial was, finished, they completed a questionnaire and were debriefed.

## Results

There was no evidence that the type of presentation (split-screen versus full-screen) had a differential effect on the verdicts of the role-playing jurors. Since the verdict data could be analyzed in several ways, we used the legal criterion employed in

### TABLE 6.1
**Summary of Verdict Responses for Jurors Exposed to Split-Screen and Full-Screen Presentations**

|              | Clark Neg | Both Neg | Clark Not Neg |
|--------------|-----------|----------|---------------|
| Split-screen | 11        | 12       |               |
| Full-screen  | 15        | 16       |               |

$X^2 = < 1, p > .05$

most of our studies; i.e., we placed responses indicating that Clark was solely negligent in one category (finding for the plaintiffs) and responses indicating that Clark was not negligent or that both Clark and Nugent were negligent in the other category (finding for the defendant). As Table 6.1 shows, the chi-square for this analysis did not approach significance. Thus, the type of presentation did not systematically influence juror verdicts in this case.

The data concerning amount of award were analyzed in two ways: first, we compared only those full-screen and split-screen jurors who stipulated an award for Mr and Mrs Nugent; second, we compared the mean awards for all jurors in the full-screen and split-screen conditions, including those jurors who did not stipulate an award.

For the first analysis, the mean awards to Mr Nugent were $3,137 in the split-screen condition and $2,919 in the full-screen condition. Comparison of these means yielded a $t$ of less than one, which, of course, failed to approach statistical significance. Mrs Nugent received a mean award of $21,200 in the split-screen condition and a mean award of $19,308 in the full-screen condition. Again, the $t$ for the comparison of these two means is less than one and is not significant.

For all jurors in the two conditions, including those who did not stipulate an award, the mean award for Mr Nugent in the split-screen condition was $1,569, while the mean award in the full-screen condition was $1,459. Mrs Nugent received a mean award of $10,000 in the split-screen condition and a mean award of $8,097 in the full-screen condition. Both the comparison of Mr Nugent's awards and Mrs Nugent's awards yielded $t$'s of less than one.

Thus, there is no evidence whatsoever that the type of presentation to which jurors were exposed affected the amount of award granted. To be sure, the mean award is consistently somewhat higher in the split-screen condition, but the variance in the amount of award within each condition is so high that this difference is readily attributable to chance fluctuations, as the $t$-values for each of the comparisons indicate.

Although there is some indication that the type of presentation may have influenced juror perceptions of attorney credibility, the evidence is less than overwhelming, since the difference is significant for only one of the attorneys. The plaintiffs' attorney received a mean credibility rating of 5.19 in the split-screen condition and a mean rating of 4.81 in the full-screen condition. The comparison of these means yielded a significant $t$ of 2.23 ($p < .05$), indicating that the plaintiffs' attorney was rated significantly more credible by those jurors who saw him on the split-screen system. By contrast, the mean credibility ratings for the defense attorney were 5.47 in the split-screen and 5.12 in the full-screen condition. While the resultant $t$ of 1.75 has a p-value of less than .10, it does not reach the .05 level required for significance.

We had assumed that the greater detail provided by the split-screen system might result in more favorable perceptions of the attorneys, especially since both were skilled courtroom performers. Although admittedly speculative, there is a possible explanation for the fact that this effect was more pronounced for the plaintiffs' than for the defense attorney. As a result of informally observing the two attorneys, we concluded that the latter's strongest rhetorical tool was his vocal dynamism and power, while the former's primary rhetorical strength seemed to lie in his expressive nonverbal behaviors and his skillful use of props such as his glasses. Obviously, such nonverbal talents could be observed more easily on the split-screen while the vocal abilities of the defense attorney would be readily recognized in both conditions.

Hence, we believe that the credibility of a skilled trial lawyer may be enhanced by the split-screen system, at least when relatively inexpensive equipment is used. Of course, if the single-screen shot could be magnified by means of a projection system, this difference might be eliminated. Moreover, we have no data to suggest whether the converse is also true; i.e., that a relatively unskilled attorney would profit from the loss of detail that occurs with the full-screen system.

This study provides no evidence that the type of presentation exercised an effect on juror retention of trial-related information. Jurors in both conditions had relatively high mean retention scores: of a possible score of 39, the means for jurors in the split-screen and full-screen conditions were 30.70 and 31.03 respectively, a difference resulting in a $t$ of less than 1. Thus, we conclude that there is no reason to expect that one system or the other is superior in terms of juror retention of trial-related information.

In terms of juror interest and motivation, there is no clear evidence that the two modes of presentation were differentially effective. The mean rating of juror interest and motivation was 5.31 in the split-screen condition and 4.94 in the full-screen condition. Although the resultant $t$ of 1.52 has a p-value of less than .10, it is not significant at the .05 level. Thus, while there is a trend toward higher self-report ratings of interest and motivation in the split-screen condition, we cannot conclude that these jurors were more motivated or found the task more interesting.

It is worth noting that the maximum possible rating of interest and motivation was 7.00. Consequently, jurors in both conditions reported that their interest and motivation were well above the midpoint (3.50) of the scale. This fact suggests that neither group found the task of viewing a videotaped trial unmotivating or uninteresting, a conclusion that bodes well for the use of either system in actual trial situations.

**Discussion**

Save for perceptions of attorney credibility, the two taping systems do not appear to produce differential effects on the juror responses measured in this study. There are, however, some admitted problems in failing to reject the null hypothesis — i.e., the hypothesis of no differences between the two groups on the variables measured. Specifically, we cannot specify a significance level for our findings of no differences, as we can in the one instance where the two conditions differed significantly. Many possible sources of error may have contributed to our failure to observe differences between groups: errors associated with the measuring instrument, errors stemming from characteristics of the jurors themselves, and so forth. Still, we developed our instruments carefully and were careful to keep the administration of the trial stimulus as constant as possible in both conditions. Even though we have as much confidence in this study as we do in most studies that support the null hypothesis, and a good deal more than we have in some, a decision was made to execute a modified replication.

## FULL-SCREEN VERSUS SPLIT-SCREEN TRIALS: A MODIFIED REPLICATION

As mentioned earlier, we were somewhat perplexed about the credibility finding for the plaintiffs' attorney. Although the difference in perceived credibility ratings may be attributable to his skillful use of props such as his glasses, numerous plausible explanations suggest themselves. One of these explanations hinges upon the physical attractiveness of the attorneys. Numerous studies (e.g., Bryne et al., 1968; Berscheid and Walster, 1969; Dion et al., 1972) have demonstrated that people respond differently to individuals who vary in physical attractiveness. In general, these responses fall in line with favorable stereotypes of attractive persons, although some of them appear to be sex-specific. Conceivably, the attractiveness of the two attorneys exerted some influence upon juror perceptions of attorney credibility.

Given the greater detail provided by the split-screen system, the effects of physical attractiveness might be more pronounced for jurors viewing trials taped using this presentation format. This reasoning, of course, is predicated upon the assumption that physical attractiveness judgments are based primarily upon facial characteristics. It is equally plausible that jurors might be more influenced by the physiques of the attorneys, which would be more visible in a full-screen trial presentation.

The following research questions were addressed in this study:

(1) Are there differences in verdicts between jurors exposed to full-screen and split-screen trials?

(2) Are there differences in perceptions of attorneys' physical attractiveness between jurors exposed to full-screen and split-screen trials?

(3) Are there differences in assessments of the effectiveness of attorneys' nonverbal communication between jurors exposed to full-screen and split-screen trials?

(4) Are there differences in perceptions of attorney credibility between jurors exposed to full-screen and split-screen trials?

## Procedures

The full-screen and split-screen videotaped versions of the trial concerning a defendant accused of conversion of bank funds, discussed in Chapter 5, was used in this study. As was mentioned earlier, two different video systems were used to tape this reenacted trial. One system consisted of a fixed color camera which produced a panoramic view of the courtroom proceedings that could be played to jurors in black-and-white or color. The trial was simultaneously taped using a fixed four-camera monochromatic system. One camera was focused upon the witness stand, one on the plaintiff's attorney when he was seated, one on the defendant's attorney when he was seated, and one on the podium where either attorney would stand when questioning a witness. A special effects generator was integrated into this system to enable us to record a shot in which the interrogating attorney occupied one-half of the screen and the witness being questioned the remaining half. The shots produced of each of the trial participants were of the upper one-third of their bodies.

The trial contained six instances of inadmissible materials. Each time the attorney who was seated off-camera raised an objection, the camera focused upon him was activated remotely by the technician manning the special effects generator. This technique produced an image in which the objecting attorney appeared in one-half of the screen and the interrogating attorney in the other half, thus ensuring that jurors would be able to pick up many subtle nuances in facial expression and gesture of the trial witnesses and the interrogating attorney. The system had the additional advantage of ensuring that jurors could observe the nonverbal behavior of both attorneys when objections were raised.

This split-screen system has the same limitations of the split-screen system used in the first study. It also has one additional limitation that merits consideration. The trial judge only appeared on camera at the beginning of the trial, to instruct the jury concerning the litigation that was before the court, and at the end of the trial, to instruct the jury concerning its deliberation and verdict. The panoramic view of the judge convening the trial and giving instructions recorded on the color system was edited in black-and-white onto the tape produced by the monochromatic system. Consequently, the judge's opening statement and instructions were exactly the same for the jurors who viewed the full-screen version and those who viewed the split-screen version of the trial.

### Experimental Design

A simple two condition design was employed in this study. The first condition consisted of a full-screen presentation and the second condition was the split-screen presentation of the trial.

### Role-Playing Jurors

Because of limitations in the availability of a courtroom setting and actual impaneled jurors, seventy-two undergraduate students at Michigan State University role-played jurors in this study. Participants were randomly assigned to one of the two experimental conditions. They were told they would be viewing an actual videotaped trial and that their task was to role-play a conscientious juror. They were instructed to assume that their verdict would be binding upon the plaintiff and the defendant.

### Measurement Techniques

The scales used in this study were the same as those used in the editing methods study (Chapter 5) with several modifications. First, there were no measures of distraction taken in this study. Second, measures of student perceptions of the physical attractiveness of the trial attorneys were taken utilizing a seven-interval semantic differential scale bounded by the choices "very physically attractive" and "very physically unattractive". The final difference concerned the use of nonverbal communication by the attorneys. A five-alternative Likert scale was employed to measure student assessments of the effectiveness of the nonverbal behavior of each attorney.

## Results

A chi-square was computed to determine if there were statistically significant differences in verdicts between role-playing jurors exposed to the full-screen presentation and those exposed to the split-screen version. There was no significant difference at the .05 level (Table 6.2), which was used for all statistical tests reported here.

Perceptions of the physical attractiveness of both attorneys were measured. Differences in ratings of physical attractiveness between students in the split-screen and full-screen conditions were tested utilizing $t$-tests. The results of these tests, presented in Table 6.3, produced no statistically significant differences.

Role-playing jurors in both the full-screen and split-screen conditions were asked to assess the effectiveness of the nonverbal communication of both attorneys (Table 6.4). There was no significant difference for the plaintiff's attorney, but there was for the defendant's attorney. Specifically, role-playing jurors in the full-screen condition evaluated the defense attorney's nonverbal communication as more effective than did their counterparts in the split-screen condition.

Assessments of the credibility of both attorneys were measured using a combination of semantic differential scales developed by Berlo et al. (1969-1970) and McCroskey (1966). Measures were obtained for the following three dimensions: (1) trustworthiness, (2) expertise, and (3) dynamism. The

### TABLE 6.2
### Verdicts in Split-Screen and Full-Screen Presentations

|  | Split-Screen | Full-Screen |
|---|---|---|
| Innocent | 25 | 19 |
| Guilty | 11 | 17 |

$X^2 = 1.46$, p $>$ .05

### TABLE 6.3
### Perceptions of the Physical Attractiveness of the Contesting Attorneys

|  | Split-Screen | Full-Screen |
|---|---|---|
| Plaintiff's attorney | 4.11 | 4.14* |
| Defense attorney | 4.39 | 4.19** |

*$t$, plaintiff's attorney = $<$ 1, df = 70, p $>$ .05 (two-tailed test).
**$t$, defense attorney = 1.02, df = 70, p $>$ .05 (two-tailed test).

### TABLE 6.4
### Assessments of the Nonverbal Communication Effectiveness of the Contesting Attorneys

|  | Split-Screen | Full-Screen |
|---|---|---|
| Plaintiff's attorney | 3.17 | 3.39* |
| Defense attorney | 2.97 | 3.53** |

*$t$, plaintiff's attorney = 1.22, df = 70, p $>$ .05 (two-tailed test).
**$t$, defense attorney = 3.04, df = 70, p $<$ .05 (two-tailed test).

responses of role-playing jurors to the items germane to each of these dimensions were factor analyzed and items loading .55 and above on a given factor without a cross-loading on another factor greater than .31 were retained. None of the factor loadings for the expertise items satisfied this criterion, indicating that perceptions of the credibility of the trial attorneys were based primarily on the trustworthiness and dynamism dimensions. The factor loadings for the items relevant to these dimensions ranged from .57 to .91.

A series of $t$-tests were used to determine if the mode of presentation systematically influenced perceptions of the trustworthiness and dynamism of either the defense attorney or the plaintiff's attorney. The results presented in Table 6.5 indicated that the perceived credibility of the attorneys did not significantly differ as a function of the mode of presentation.

## Discussion

The results warrant two conclusions: first, exposure to the two modes of presentation does have some systematic effect upon juror perceptions of trial attorneys; second, exposure to either mode of presentation does not significantly influence the

**TABLE 6.5**
**Perceptions of the Credibility of the Contesting Attorneys***

|  |  | *Split-Screen* | *Full-Screen* |
|---|---|---|---|
| Plaintiff's attorney | trustworthiness | 26.06 | 25.65 |
|  | dynamism | 25.67 | 26.53 |
| Defense attorney | trustworthiness | 25.03 | 25.61 |
|  | dynamism | 25.92 | 27.53 |

*$t$- values $<1$ for all comparisons save the dynamism of the defense attorney, $t = 1.33$, df = 70, p $>$.05 (two-tailed test).

verdicts arrived at by jurors. Although perceptions of attorney credibility and physical attractiveness were not influenced by these alternative modes of presentation, assessments of the effectiveness of the defense attorney's nonverbal communication were affected. Specifically, role-playing jurors exposed to the full-screen trial presentation found the defense attorney's nonverbal communication to be more effective than did their counterparts who viewed the split-screen presentation. This may be attributable to the use of very expressive hand gestures employed by the defense attorney to emphasize important issues during his questioning of witnesses and during his closing arguments, which were more discernible in the full-screen presentation.

It should be noted that this finding varies from the results of our first study, in which we observed that the credibility ratings of one of the attorneys were higher in the split-screen condition. Taken together, the two studies suggest that differences in the communication styles of trial participants produce situations where one presentational format is more effective than others. Stated differently, the rhetorical strengths of some attorneys may be accentuated by the split-screen system, while others may profit from full-screen taping. Though this conclusion is far from earth-shaking, it underscores the difficulty involved in making sovereign gereralizations about the impact of one system or the other on juror perceptions of trial participants.

Even though this difference in dynamism materialized, it should be noted that verdict decisions were not significantly influenced by the two different modes of presentation. Consequently, the results of this study, considered with those from the first study, provide no substantial evidence that suggests the superiority of one video system over the other. Simply stated, the use of either recording system produces essentially the same verdict results.

## JUROR RESPONSES TO VARYING CAMERA SHOTS

A basic question regarding the use of videotaped trial

materials concerns the type of camera shot that should be employed when videotaping a witness. Currently, three types of camera shots are predominantly used in the legal system when videotaping witness testimony: (1) the close-up shot, which provides a tight focus on the head and shoulders of the witness; (2) the medium shot, which focuses from the head to just above the waist of the witness; and, (3) the long shot, which provides full focus of the witness from head to foot. In addition, a very long shot is often used at the beginning of a taping session to allow the jurors to see all of the participants. The purpose of this study was to determine whether the three different types of camera shots exert any systematic influence upon juror impressions of witnesses.

Millerson (1964) summarizes the utility of each of these shots from a production perspective. The long shot serves to personalize the individual(s) being filmed. In contrast to long shots (e.g., the very long shot), movement becomes more recognizable. Moreover, facial expressions and gestures become more dominant because more emphasis is placed on the actor(s) than the setting in which the action transpires.

The medium shot serves to focus attention upon one or two individuals within a setting. Facial expressions and gestures are more prominent in a medium than in a long shot.

The purpose of the closeup shot is to concentrate the viewer's attention on details that might otherwise be overlooked. This type of shot is normally used for dramatic emphasis of specific detail (Madsen, 1973). Facial expressions are very prominent when a closeup shot is used.

Research examining the effects of different types of camera shots in nonlegal settings has produced some interesting results. Williams (1965) examined the effect of varying camera shots on viewers' expressed interest level toward a televised lecture. His results indicated that expressed interest level did not significantly differ as a result of using a variety of closeup and long shots compared to utilizing a static medium shot. However, when examining shot differences using a film screen,

Williams (1968) found that the expressed interest level of viewers significantly decreased when a long shot was employed.

Wurtzel and Dominick (1971-1972) examined the effects of acting style and camera shot on viewers' evaluations of television drama. An eleven-minute emotional scene was performed by three professional actors utilizing two different acting styles: film acting and stage acting. Stage acting differs from film acting in that gestures and expressions are more elaborate and pronounced. The scene was filmed four times in order to obtain the levels of the two independent variables of acting style (film acting and stage acting) and type of shot (closeup and medium). Viewers evaluated the scene more favorably when the actors were film acting and a closeup shot was used as opposed to a medium shot. Viewers in the medium shot condition evaluated the scene more favorably than did viewers in the closeup shot condition when stage acting was employed.

McCain and Repensky (1972) examined the effect of camera shot on interpersonal attraction. Two comedians, Edmonds and Curly, performed two routines which were taped using three camera shots: a closeup, medium, and long shot. The measure of interpersonal attraction included three independent dimensions: physical attraction, social attraction, and task attraction.

Results indicated that camera shot does affect interpersonal attraction, but the effects differed for each performer. Analysis of the physical attractiveness data yielded a significant main effect for comedian and a significant interaction for comedian and camera shot. Edmonds was perceived as being more physically attractive than Curly in the closeup shot, while Curly was perceived as being more physically attractive than Edmonds in the medium and long shots. No significant differences were obtained for social attractiveness, but a significant interaction was observed for task attractiveness. Curly was perceived as most task attractive in the closeup condition while Edmonds was perceived as least task attractive in the closeup condition.

The two comedians did not differ in task attractiveness in any other condition.

Clearly, some characteristics of the two comedians interacted with camera shot, but it is difficult to determine just what they were. The authors offer a number of plausible explanations which include the roles of the comedians (i.e., straight-man versus funny-man), their physical appearance, and the quality of their performances.

McCain and Divers (1973) examined the effects of body type, sex of the source, and camera shot on interpersonal attraction and source credibility. Three males and three females were selected as stimulus persons and were classified into three categories of body type (Sheldon, 1954): endomorph (fat or plump); mesomorph (muscular or athletic); and ectomorph (thin or skinny). A closeup shot, a medium shot, and a long shot were employed. Interpersonal attraction was composed of three independent dimensions: physical attraction, social attraction, and task attraction; while source credibility included five independent dimensions: competence, sociability, dynamism, composure, and character. The six stimulus persons delivered a "three minute neutral speech," which was taped utilizing three cameras simultaneously in order to obtain the three levels of camera shot.

Data analysis yielded significant main effects for body type and sex of source. No main effect for camera shot was found, but a number of significant interactions were obtained. The interpretation of these results is clouded by the lack of control in the study. For example, the results suggested that the sex of the speaker had a strong impact on the dependent measures, but the authors suggested the findings must be interpreted cautiously:

> Since only one person of each sex represented each body type, the differences are really personal attribute differences of single individuals. Facial expression, fluency of presentation and other nonverbal variations between the males and females may well provide better explanations for differences between them than their gender differences [McCain and Divers, 1973: 9-10].

Simply stated, a host of other source characteristics not controlled for or measured by have produced the findings observed.

One additional point merits comment. In the studies reviewed thus far, the role of the sources differed; sources served as comedians (McCain and Repensky, 1972), lecturers (Williams, 1965, 1968), actors (Wurtzel and Dominick, 1971-1972), and neutral speakers (McCain and Divers, 1973). Conceivably, as the relationship between the source and the viewer changes, different cues emitted by the source become salient for the viewer. Certainly, the role relationship between jurors and witnesses is a relatively unique one. Consequently, results of this prior research may not be directly applicable to the legal setting, emphasizing the need for research on the effects of different camera shots on juror perceptions of different types of witnesses.

Although the generalization of these findings to the legal setting is questionable, they do provide a useful framework for the development of hypotheses. A number of hypotheses were developed with the aid of this framework. Hypotheses concerning the main effects for witness type were developed first and then modified to take into account the potential effects of the different camera shots. Although many different witness types could have been incorporated into this study, we restricted ourselves to strong and weak witnesses.

The first variable considered was the perceived composure of a witness. Composure is used here as a measure of the general presentational style, both verbal and nonverbal, of a witness. Research on speech fluency indicates that an inverse relationship exists between a source's speech fluency and the amount of anxiety he or she is perceived to be experiencing (Dibner, 1956; Krause and Pilisuk, 1961; Pope and Siegman, 1962; Zimbardo et al., 1963; Kasl and Mahl, 1965; Cook, 1969). Individuals who appear to be experiencing high levels of anxiety are generally not perceived as being composed. It is reasonable to assume that a strong witness's testimony would be presented in a fluent manner and he or she would be assertive, attentive, and unhesitant while testifying. A weak witness, on the other hand, would be nonfluent, uncertain, fumbling, and inattentive. This reasoning led to the development of the following hypothesis which, in essence, constitutes an assessment of our manipulation of witness presentational style:

(1) A strong witness will be perceived as more composed than a weak witness.

The perceived credibility of a witness was the next variable considered. The writings of Aristotle stressed the need for good delivery in acquiring credibility (Cooper, 1932). Numerous researchers have investigated the relationship between source presentation style and perceived credibility. Using the credibility scales developed by Berlo and Lemert (1961), Miller and Hewgill (1964) and Sereno and Hawkins (1967) found that fluent sources were perceived to be significantly more dynamic and competent than non-fluent sources. Moreover, a fluent speaker was rated as significantly more trustworthy than nonfluent sources. Sereno and Hawkins (1967) report similar findings for a source's trustworthiness, although the finding was not statistically significant. Using the authority and character scales developed by McCroskey (1966) and Berlo et al. (1969-1970), the following three hypotheses were developed:

(2) A strong witness will be perceived safer (more trustworthy) than a weak witness.

(3) A strong witness will be perceived as more qualified than a weak witness.

(4) A strong witness will be perceived as more dynamic than a weak witness.

The potential effects of presentation style on perceptions of witness authority and character were also considered. Measures for these two variables were developed by McCroskey (1966) and are considered to be related to the dimensions of credibility derived by other researchers. In light of this relationship, the presentational style of a source should have the same effect upon these two variables as it does upon credibility. Some support for this expectation derives from the results of the study completed by McCroskey and Mehrley (1969) discussed earlier. These results suggest the following two hypotheses:

(5) A strong witness will be perceived as more authoritative than a weak witness.

(6) A strong witness will be perceived as having higher character than a weak witness.

The presentation style of a witness might also influence the amount of trial-related information retained by jurors. The fumbling nonverbal behaviors and nonfluent speech of the weak witness may distract jurors, causing them to attend more to these cues than to the testimony presented. This reasoning is supported to some extent by the findings from prior studies, mentioned in Chapter 5, investigating the relationship between distraction and message recall, even though their results are somewhat inconsistent. Specifically, some researchers have reported that distraction decreases recall of message content (Vohs, 1964; Gardner, 1966; Haaland and Venkatesan, 1968), while others have reported just the opposite effect (Silverman and Regula, 1968).

As noted in the preceding chapter, one explanation for these inconsistent findings is offered by Baron et al. (1973) who suggest that the influence of distraction on message recall depends upon whether or not the distraction can be ignored. Message recipients may be able to ignore mild distractions and attend to message content; however, more intense distractions may be difficult to ignore reducing the amount of attention devoted to message content. Assuming that a weak witness's presentation style is more than mildly distracting, the following hypothesis was posited:

(7) Jurors exposed to a weak witness will retain less trial-related information than jurors exposed to a strong witness.

Continuing with the same line of reasoning, witness presentation style may have an effect on juror interest in the proceedings. While many factors influence a message recipient's interest in a source's message, one general relationship is obvious: the more skillfully a message is delivered, the greater the likelihood of arousing receiver interest. Since a strong witness's presentation style is more skillful than that of a weak witness, the following hypothesis was generated:

(8) Jurors exposed to a strong witness will express greater interest in the proceedings than jurors exposed to a weak witness.

Thus far, the hypotheses have focused on the relationship between witness type and the dependent variables without considering the potential effects of varying camera shots. Those effects will now be discussed and the hypotheses will be modified to account for them.

Earlier, it was suggested that the number of sensory cues provided for a viewer's consumption is determined to a large extent by the type of shot used to videotape a message source. Specifically, the number of sensory cues provided would be greatest in the long shot and least in the closeup shot, with the medium shot falling between the two. The cues presented would be most salient in the closeup shot, less salient in the medium, and least salient in the long shot. Assuming facial affect cues will have more impact on juror perceptions of witnesses than will other nonverbal cues, a strong witness might be evaluated most favorably in a long shot. The pattern of evaluations would be reversed for a weak witness since facial affect cues indicative of anxiety, uncertainty, and inattentiveness would be least obvious in the long shot, more obvious in the medium shot, and most obvious in the closeup shot.

Given this line of reasoning, we hypothesized that juror perceptions of a strong witness's composure, safety, qualification, dynamism, authority, and character would be most favorable in a closeup shot, less favorable in a medium shot, and least favorable in a long shot. Two additional hypotheses concerning the amount of trial-related information retained by jurors and their interest in the proceedings were developed. Specifically, we expected the amount of information retained to be greatest among jurors exposed to a closeup shot of the strong witness and least for jurors exposed to a long shot, with jurors exposed to a medium shot falling in between. The same pattern for juror interest in the proceedings was hypothesized.

Finally, a general interaction hypothesis logically followed from these theoretical expectations: juror perceptions of a strong witness will be more favorable in the closeup shot, while juror perceptions of a weak witness will be more favorable in the long shot.

## Procedures

With the aid of legal experts, a transcript of an actual deposition was selected of a defendant who was accused of negligence resulting in an industrial accident. The deposition, approximately thirty minutes in length, consisted of cross-examination by the plaintiff's attorney but did not contain direct examination by the defense attorney. Professional actors played the roles of the witness and the defense attorney while an actual attorney assumed the role of the plaintiff's attorney.

The type of witness manipulation consisted of the same actor playing two different roles: a strong witness and a weak witness. The presentation style of the strong witness was characterized as fluent, assertive, and attentive as contrasted with the weak witness who was uncertain, hesitant, fumbling, and inattentive.

The actor was trained to exhibit verbal and nonverbal cues that would engender impressions of the presentation styles of interest. For example, for the strong witness role, the actor was instructed to speak normally, fluently, and with confidence; to hold his head erect; to maintain eye contact with the questioning attorney, and to lean slightly toward him. He was also directed to relax and not fidget, tap his feet, or place his arms akimbo. For the weak witness role, the actor was asked to speak softly and nonfluently, insert pauses — "um's" and "uh's" in his sentences — maintain low eye contact with the questioning attorney, and lean slightly away from him. Additionally, he was instructed to tense his muscles slightly, sigh occasionally, fidget, and tap his fingers and feet. These behaviors are indicative of the presentation styles of interest (Dibner, 1956; Krause and Pilisuk, 1961; Reece and Whitman, 1962; Pope and Siegman, 1962; Zimbardo et al. 1963; Kasl and Mahl, 1965; Dittman and Llewellyn, 1968; Cook, 1969; Mehrabian, 1969, 1971a; Harrison, 1974).

*Taping the Witness*

The deposition was videotaped in color in a television studio at Michigan State University with the participants seated at a rectangular table in front of a plain backdrop. The witness was seated at the middle of the table, with the attorneys at the ends. Three cameras were used simultaneously to achieve the three levels of camera shot which contained only the witness. A fourth camera shot (a very long shot), containing the witness and both attorneys, was recorded and edited onto the beginning and end of the tapes to offer the viewer a sense of location.

The angle used for all camera shots was ninety degrees to the vertical plane. This angle was selected because past research has demonstrated that deviations from this angle have biasing effects on viewers (Tiemens, 1970; McCain and Wakshlag, 1974; McCain et al., 1977). The deposition was videotaped twice, once for each witness type, and the testimony was identical in both presentations save for the difference in delivery style.

*Trial Synopsis*

To provide a context for the deposition, a brief trial summary was written with the assistance of legal experts. In addition, an injury for the plaintiff was contrived since the original deposition did not mention the specific injury suffered. A moderately serious injury was desirable to avoid influencing juror impressions of the witness which might be attributable to the injury sustained.

Identification of a moderately serious injury was achieved by presenting ninety-eight undergraduate students a list of twenty-five injuries the plaintiff could have sustained. They were asked to rate each injury on a seven-point scale, ranging from "not serious" to "very serious." A broken leg with no additional complications was used in the study since it was rated as a moderately serious injury.

## Role-Playing Jurors

The role-playing jurors who participated in this study were 197 undergraduate students enrolled in communication courses at Michigan State University. The students were told they were participating in a jury size study and after hearing trial testimony they would be assigned to juries for deliberation. The trial synopsis was then read to them followed by a presentation of the videotaped deposition. After viewing the deposition, the students completed a questionnaire, were informed they would not be deliberating, and were debriefed.

## Measurement Techniques

This study was designed to evaluate the effects of camera shot and type of witness upon juror perceptions of the witness's composure, credibility (safety, qualification, and dynamism), authority, and character, the amount of information retained by jurors, and juror interest in the proceedings.

Juror perceptions of the witness's composure were measured with ten seven-point Likert-type scales. The adjectives used were: friendly-unfriendly, confident-unconfident, relaxed-tense, attentive-inattentive, assertive-nonassertive, poised-nervous, calm-anxious, comfortable-uncomfortable, unhesitant-hesitant and outgoing-reserved.

A factor analysis of the data collected using these items yielded a single factor solution. One item (friendly-unfriendly) failed to load adequately and was deleted from the scale. A reliability test of the remaining nine items produced an alpha coefficient of .90.

Witness credibility was measured using the scales developed by Berlo et al. (1969-1970). This measure consisted of fifteen seven-point Likert-type scales, which theoretically comprise three dimensions of credibility: safety, qualification, and dynamism.

The data collected employing these scales were factor analyzed using the multiple-group method (Nunnally, 1967). The results of this analysis indicated that juror credibility assessments were indeed based upon the dimensions of safety, qualification, and dynamism. Reliability assessments of these dimensions produced alpha coefficents of .72, .72, and .85 respectively.

Juror perceptions of the witness's authority and character were measured utilizing scales developed by McCroskey (1966). Twenty-two of these items measured character assessments and consisted of character statements about the witness to which jurors rated their level of agreement or disagreement, while twenty items concerned the authority assessment.

The forty-two items were factor analyzed to a two factor solution using varimax rotation with communalities in the diagonal. The results indicated that a number of items failed to load adequately, given a loading criterion of no less than .50 on one factor and no more than .20 on the other. After eliminating those items which failed to meet this criterion, the authority scale consisted of seven items and the character scale ten items. The resulting alpha coefficients for the authority and character scales were .85 and .90, respectively.

The amount of information retained by jurors was measured in the following manner. Sixty-four multiple choice questions were constructed concerning the testimony presented and were pretested using fifty-eight undergraduate students enrolled in communication courses at Michigan State University. The respondents were divided into equal groups. One group was shown the medium shot of the strong witness while the other was shown the medium shot of the weak witness. After viewing the videotape, they completed a questionnaire which included the sixty-four information retention items. The items were dichotomously coded as right or wrong and subjected to an item analysis. Eighteen of the items demonstrated low reliabilities and were eliminated; a reliability test of the remaining forty-six items produced an alpha coefficent of .89.

Juror interest was measured using a three item scale which yielded an alpha coefficient of .70.

## Results

The results will be discussed for each dependent measure. Two-way analyses of variance were used to test the effects of camera shot and witness type upon each of the dependent variables. The Newman-Keuls procedure was employed for comparisons among cell means and the .05 level of significance was used for all statistical tests.

### Composure

Table 6.6 contains the mean composure ratings of the witness by jurors in the six conditions. The analysis revealed both an interpretable main effect for witness type ($F = 170.08$, $p < .05$) and an interpretable interaction between type of shot and witness type ($F = 4.43$, $p < .05$). Both of these effects are interpretable because the interaction is ordinal (Keppell, 1973). The presentation style of witnesses significantly influenced juror ratings of

**TABLE 6.6**
**Mean Composure Ratings of the Witness by Jurors
in the Six Conditions***

|  | Strong Witness | Weak Witness |
| --- | --- | --- |
| Closeup | $37.33_a$ | $28.53_b$ |
| Medium | $37.74_a$ | $22.78_c$ |
| Long | $39.62_a$ | $24.37_c$ |

*Means labeled with a common letter do not differ significantly.

witness composure such that the strong witness was perceived as more composed than the weak witness.

The results of the Newman-Keuls test indicated that significant differences existed between strong and weak witnesses across all three types of shots and accounted for a substantial amount of the variance in the composure measure ($n^2 = .50$). The significant interaction between witness type and shot type accounted for a limited amount of variance ($n^2 = .03$) and was primarily attributable to the weak witness's perceived composure in the closeup condition.

## Qualification

Perceptions of the witness's qualification were also significantly affected by the presentation style of the witness (F = 4.59, p < .05). Inspection of the means (Table 6.7) for this main effect reveals that the strong witness was perceived as more qualified than the weak witness in all three camera shots.

The results of the Newman-Keuls test indicated, however, that only the ratings between the strong and the weak witnesses in the closeup shot were significantly different. Moreover, the main effect only accounted for 3% of the variance in the perceived qualification of witnesses.

### TABLE 6.7
### Mean Qualification Ratings of the Witness by Jurors
### in the Six Conditions*

|         | Strong Witness | Weak Witness |
|---------|---------------|--------------|
| Closeup | $24.37_a$     | $22.04_b$    |
| Medium  | $23.44_{ab}$  | $22.85_{ab}$ |
| Long    | $23.81_{ab}$  | $22.92_{ab}$ |

*Means labeled with a common letter do not differ significantly.

## Dynamism

A significant main effect was observed for witness type in this analysis (F = 205.44, p < .05). As Table 6.8 indicates, the strong witness was consistently perceived as more dynamic than the weak witness across the three types of camera shots. The amount of variance in dynamism accounted for by this factor was substantial ($n^2$ = .40).

## Information Retention

The analysis for this dependent measure produced a significant main effect for witness type (F = 3.99, p < .05) and a significant interaction (F = 4.23, p < .05); however, only the interaction is interpretable since it is disordinal (Keppell, 1973). An inspection of the means contained in Table 6.9 indicates that role-playing jurors in the closeup and medium shot conditions retained more information from the strong witness than did their counterparts exposed to the weak witness in the same shot conditions.

There was no significant difference in information retention between jurors exposed to the strong witness and those viewing the weak witness in the long shot conditions. However, role-playing jurors who viewed a long shot of the weak witness retained significantly more information than their counterparts in the closeup and medium shot conditions. This interaction accounted for 5% of the variance in the information retention measure.

## Interest

Juror interest in the proceedings was significantly influenced only by the presentation style of the witness (F = 18.33, p < .05). Role-playing jurors expressed greater interest in the proceedings when exposed to a strong witness rather than a weak witness, although results of the Newman-Keuls test indicated only interest ratings in the closeup and medium shots were significantly different (Table 6.10). Assessment of the strength of the relationship indicated a moderate effect ($n^2$ = .10).

### TABLE 6.8
### Mean Dynamism Ratings of the Witness by Jurors
### in the Six Conditions*

|          | Strong Witness      | Weak Witness       |
|----------|---------------------|--------------------|
| Closeup  | $19.48_a$           | $14.89_b$          |
| Medium   | $19.88_a$           | $14.15_b$          |
| Long     | $20.11_a$           | $13.59_b$          |

*Means labeled with a common letter do not differ significantly.

### TABLE 6.9
### Mean Retention Scores for Jurors in the Six Conditions*

|          | Strong Witness      | Weak Witness       |
|----------|---------------------|--------------------|
| Closeup  | $36.89_{ac}$        | $33.26_b$          |
| Medium   | $37.74_{ac}$        | $33.00_b$          |
| Long     | $34.70_{abc}$       | $36.85_c$          |

*Means labeled with a common letter do not differ significantly.

### TABLE 6.10
### Mean Ratings of Juror Interest for the Six Conditions*

|          | Strong Witness      | Weak Witness       |
|----------|---------------------|--------------------|
| Closeup  | $14.56_a$           | $11.92_b$          |
| Medium   | $15.07_a$           | $11.81_b$          |
| Long     | $14.07_a$           | $13.33_{ab}$       |

*Means labeled with a common letter do not differ significantly.

### TABLE 6.11
### Mean Safety Ratings of the Witness by Jurors
### in the Six Conditions*

|         | Strong Witness | Weak Witness |
|---------|----------------|--------------|
| Closeup | 21.22          | 21.52        |
| Medium  | 21.96          | 20.89        |
| Long    | 21.26          | 21.37        |

*No means differ significantly.

### TABLE 6.12
### Mean Authoritativeness Ratings of the Witness
### by Jurors in the Six Conditions*

|         | Strong Witness | Weak Witness |
|---------|----------------|--------------|
| Closeup | $19.92_a$      | $17.63_{ac}$ |
| Medium  | $18.66_{ab}$   | $16.03_c$    |
| Long    | $16.77_{bc}$   | $18.15_{ac}$ |

*Means labeled with a common letter do not differ significantly.

### TABLE 6.13
### Mean Character Ratings of the Witness by Jurors
### in the Six Conditions*

|         | Strong Witness | Weak Witness |
|---------|----------------|--------------|
| Closeup | 35.26          | 33.93        |
| Medium  | 34.74          | 34.56        |
| Long    | 33.15          | 34.44        |

*No means differ significantly.

## Safety

Table 6.11 contains the mean safety ratings for jurors in the six conditions. Juror ratings on the safety dimension of the credibility measure were not significantly influenced by the presentation style of the witness nor by the type of shot used to videotape the witness (F $=$ $<$ 1, p $>$.05 for both effects).

## Authority

Data analyses for this variable indicated that type of shot interacted with witness presentation style and systematically influenced juror perceptions of witness authority (F $=$ 3.29, p $<$.05, see means in Table 6.12). The strong witness was perceived as more authoritative than the weak witness in the closeup and medium shots. However, the weak witness was rated more authoritative than the strong witness in the long shot. The Newman-Keuls test revealed no significant differences for the weak witness across the three camera shots while the strong witness was perceived as significantly more authoritative in the closeup than in the long shot. Moreover, there were significant differences between the ratings of the weak witness in the medium shot and those of the strong witness in the medium and closeup shot conditions. This interaction accounted for only 4% of the variance in this dependent measure.

## Character

Table 6.13 contains the mean character ratings of the witness by jurors in the six conditions. No significant differences in character ratings attributable to witness type or shot type were observed (F $=$ $<$ 1, p $>$.05 for both effects).

## Discussion

The findings supported Hypotheses 1, 3, 4, 7 and 8; the remaining hypotheses were not supported. The strong witness was perceived as more composed than the weak witness; however, the strong witness was evaluated as being more composed in the long shot while the weak witness's ratings were highest in the closeup condition.

The strong witness was generally perceived as more qualified than the weak witness, replicating findings from previous research (Miller and Hewgill, 1964; Sereno and Hawkins, 1967). This effect is primarily attributable to the significant difference in ratings between the strong and weak witness in the closeup shot condition. This outcome suggests that facial nonverbal cues clearly displayed in this shot influence credibility assessments of witnesses, at least on the qualification dimension, even though the relationship is weak.

Perceived dynamism, another dimension of credibility, was also systematically influenced by witness presentation style. The strong witness was perceived across all three types of shots as more dynamic than the weak witness. The type of shot, however, did not enhance or detract from juror ratings of dynamism for either witness type. In sum, no substantial relationships between either witness presentation style or type of shot and the three dimensions of credibility — trustworthiness, qualification (competence), and dynamism — were identified.

The amount of information retained by role-playing jurors was influenced by the interaction between witness presentation style and shot type. Jurors exposed to the strong witness in the closeup and medium shots retained significantly more information than their counterparts in the long shot condition. This trend was reversed for the weak witness, with jurors in the long shot condition retaining more information than jurors in the closeup and medium shot conditions. Moreover, role-playing jurors who viewed the strong witness in the closeup and medium shot conditions retained significantly more information than jurors exposed to the weak witness in the same shot conditions. Jurors exposed to the weak witness in the closeup and medium shot conditions may have found the witness's visible nonverbal behaviors more distracting than jurors in the long shot condition and subsequently retained less information. Even though these differences exist, the amount of variance in the dependent measure attributable to the interaction is not substantial.

Jurors exposed to the strong witness generally expressed a greater level of interest in the proceedings than those exposed to the weak witness. The more fluent presentation style of the strong witness was probably easier to comprehend and hence more interesting than the weak witness's presentation. The differences in expressed interest level may also be attributable to the perceived dynamism of the two witness types. Dynamic witnesses are probably better able to hold juror interest than witnesses who are not dynamic. Support for this explanation is evidenced by the reasonably strong correlation between dynamism and interest ($r = .30$).

The results of this study revealed a number of significant effects for witness type, but no independent effects for type of camera shot. Camera shot did interact with witness type to influence significantly perceptions of witness composure and authority. The amount of variance accounted for in the dependent variables by these interactions was not substantial. Consequently, the effects upon juror perceptions of either strong or weak witnesses will be relatively the same whether a closeup, medium, or long shot is used to videotape witness testimony.

## SUMMING UP

This chapter has presented the results of three studies investigating juror response to a limited number of production techniques. Findings from the first two studies, which examined the potential influence of different presentation formats (split-screen versus full-screen), provided no substantial evidence that would suggest the superiority of one video system over the other. The two significant findings identified in these studies involved differences in perceptions of the credibility of the plaintiffs' attorney in the first study and differences in the assessments of the effectiveness of the defense attorney's nonverbal communication in the second study. The fact that the credibility finding was not replicated in the second study suggests the existence of source by mode of presentation interactions that remain to be empirically explored. However, the lack of systematic differences in verdicts between jurors exposed to a full-screen presentation and those who viewed the split-screen version supports our conclusion that either system exerts essentially the same influence upon jurors.

The results of the third study provided no grounds for concluding that the type of camera shot used (closeup, medium, or long) would independently influence juror perceptions of witnesses. Although juror evaluations of witness composure and authority were influenced by an interaction between witness type and camera shot, the strength of these relationships was quite moderate. Therefore, the influence upon juror perceptions of either strong or weak witnesses will be relatively the same regardless of which of these shots is used.

*7*

# DETECTING DECEPTION

Witnesses often give differing accounts of events during their testimony. Much conflicting testimony probably results from honestly differing perceptions about the facts of a case. In some instances, however, conflicting testimony stems from deliberate attempts to deceive, or to put it in legal terms, from perjury. The rules of procedure governing trials are designed, in part, to help jurors fairly resolve instances of conflicting testimony. Cross-examination helps to test the credibility of witnesses thus giving jurors additional information on which to base their decisions regarding the truthfulness of testimony. The detection of deception, or lying, by witnesses is an important matter for jurors and a crucial determinant of the judicious rendering of verdicts. Indeed, a trial can be conceived of as a test of credibility where "those charged with decision-making, whether they be judges or jurors, must not only weigh the information and evidence, but must also evaluate the veracity of the opposing evidential and informational sources" (Miller and Boster, 1977: 28).

Does the mode of presenting testimony affect the ability of jurors to assess accurately the veracity of witnesses? Opponents of videotaped trials and testimony believe that it does. The following remarks capture the skepticism of some legal experts about the capabilities of videotape to present testimony in a way that enhances juror success in evaluating the demeanor of witnesses:

> The presumption behind the formal court setting and proceedings is that they have an impact on witness performance and perception, as well as on the behavior of other trial participants and observers. This is a tenable presumption, even if the precise details and mechanics of it remain a mystery. A witness who testifies out-of-court, with only counsel and perhaps a bailiff present, will not have the same psychological compulsions toward testifying accurately and completely as an in-court live witness. . . . Beyond that, *the medium cannot capture the total psychological and physical essence of a witness — persuasiveness, credibility, hesitancy, and forcefulness are indicated through arm, hand, or eye movements or other bodily changes* [Brakel, 1975: 957, emphasis supplied].

Basically, Brakel offers two arguments concerning the limitations of videotape as a medium for capturing witness testimony. His first rests on the assumption that witnesses whose testimony is videotaped outside the courtroom are more likely to testify inaccurately — though it is not entirely clear, we assume that Brakel includes both unintentional, honest inaccuracies and intentional, deceptive misstatements in his indictment. Supposedly, certain aspects of the physical and psychological milieu of the courtroom bring out the best in witnesses, causing them to recount events more accurately and completely than in noncourtroom settings.

While there is a tone of plausibility to this argument, we are unaware of any research dealing directly with it. Moreover, as is true with many of the issues explored in this volume, a persuasive argument can also be made for the opposite alternative: the stress and anxiety engendered by testifying in the courtroom may cause witnesses to forget or to repress information they would remember in the less stressful environs of an attorney's office or a taping studio. Certainly, the sanctions for perjury are not lifted when testimony is given out of court; witnesses remain aware of the penalties for fabricated testimony. Finally, though it occurs relatively infrequently, the present rules of trial procedure permit depositions of absent witnesses to be read to jurors, a procedure that not only involves taking testimony outside the courtroom but also denies the jurors any opportunity to scrutinize the witness's demeanor.

Although the questions just discussed have important implications for the trial process, our research pertains primarily to Brakel's second contention: the argument that videotape cannot capture the plethora of nonverbal and paralinguistic cues presented by the witness; cues that are *assumed* to aid jurors in arriving at accurate judgments of veracity. Such an argumentative stance is hardly surprising, since a substantial body of folklore, conventional wisdom, and social stereotyping rests on the belief that liars give themselves away by their nonverbal behaviors. As long ago as 900 B.C., a papyrus Veda described the behavior of liars thusly: "He does not answer questions, or they are evasive answers; he speaks nonsense, rubs the great toe along the ground, and shivers; his face is discolored; he rubs the roots of his hair with his fingers" [Trovillo, 1939: 849].

Despite this widely shared faith in nonverbal behavior as an aid in deception detection, a healthy skepticism seems warranted on both theoretical and empirical grounds. Even when a great deal of total information, verbal and nonverbal, is available, there is no assurance that persons will be able to perceive and assimilate it. Indeed, what may occur is information overload, causing the individual charged with making veracity assessments to block out or overlook important cues. Danowski (1974) argues that when people receive more information than they can process, they experience confusion and subsequent higher error rates. Filtering and chunking are two processing strategies receivers use to adapt to overload, and both involve the use of stereotypic conceptions to avoid coping with all the available data.

The preceding reference to stereotyping suggests a second reason why nonverbal information may mislead rather than aid in detecting deception, at least in situations where the potential deceiver is a relative stranger. The nonverbal behaviors stereotypically associated with lying — e.g., high frequency of nervous adaptors, failure to maintain eye contact, frequent nonfluency — can be triggered by a variety of antecedent motivational conditions, both organismic and situational. For instance, such nonverbal behaviors are commonplace for high communication apprehensives (McCroskey, 1977), even though their messages are totally truthful. In a situational vein, the stress-producing characteristics of the courtroom environment, mentioned earlier, may cause a witness to exhibit nonverbal displays stereotypic of lying even when the witness is testifying truthfully. Such reasoning is congruent with a drive reduction learning theory approach to motivation (Brown, 1960), which holds that drive is a generalized response energizer that can be activated by a wide range of stimuli. Furthermore, this reasoning also suggests that even if individuals can perceive and assimilate the many nonverbal behaviors bombarding them, they must also make inferences concerning the specific mediating factors leading to a particular pattern of nonverbal cues, and these inferences themselves are "chancy" guesses highly subject to error.

Nor do prior studies dealing with the ability of observers to detect deception perpetrated by relative strangers strongly support the expectation that nonverbal information enhances accuracy. for example, Maier and Thurber (1968) asked persons to lie and to tell the truth while being interviewed. Observers then evaluated the veracity of the interviewees after either watching the actual live interview, hearing a tape recording of it, or reading a transcript of the interview. The audiotape and written presentational modes resulted in greater accuracy in detecting deception (about 77% in each case) than did the live condition (58%). Maier and Thurber suggest that visual cues may distract attention from verbal and paralinguistic cues denoting lying.

The question of the role of nonverbal cues in detecting deception has several important implications for policy-makers concerned with the use of videotaped trials and depositions. If amount of nonverbal information is positively related to accuracy in detecting deception, color taping systems would seem preferable to monochromatic systems because the former medium captures more of the nonverbal cues presented by witnesses. Perhaps even more important, the maximum amount of nonverbal information available in the live setting would suggest that videotaped trial materials should be used sparingly, at least when juror assessment of witness veracity is a primary consideration. On the other hand, if amount of nonverbal information is essentially unrelated to accuracy, or if the two variables are negatively related, videotaped materials could be employed without reducing juror ability to detect deceptive testimony.

Because of our interest in these issues surrounding possible influences of presentation mode on accuracy of deception detection, the two studies reported in this chapter dealt with the following questions:

(1) In general, how accurate are observers in detecting deception on the part of relative strangers?
(2) What effects do variations in the mode of presentation have on observer ability to detect deception?
(3) What effects do various shots of the potential deceiver (head only, body only, head and body) have on observer ability to detect deception?

## EFFECTS OF PRESENTATIONAL MODE AND CAMERA SHOT ON DETECTING DECEPTION

Although both color and monochromatic videotape preserve more of the vocal and nonverbal cues of witnesses than do an audiotape and a written transcript, the two tape modes vary in the amount of nonverbal information they convey. As noted above, color tape retains more nonverbal information than black-and-white tape. This study examined the relative accuracy in detecting deception of observers exposed to color tape, monochromatic tape, audiotape, and transcript modes of presenting testimony. Research by Ekman and Friesen (1974) demonstrated that individuals display nonverbal cues which are used by observers in attempting to detect deception. The observers in Ekman and Friesen's research were able to identify deception more accurately when they observed only a deceiver's body as compared to a head only view.

This finding suggests an important question: how much of a witness's body should appear on a videotape to maximize the potential of jurors accurately detecting deceptive testimony? In the Ekman and Friesen study, observers saw only the body or the head of the deceiver. Perhaps those who saw only the body were more accurate because facial cues normally available were absent, forcing observers to be more attentive to bodily cues. If cues emanating from the head had been available for observation, they may have distracted observers from attending to leakage cues coming from the body. This study included head only, body only, and head and body conditions to evaluate this possibility.

Finally, the Ekman and Friesen (1974) study focused upon only nonverbal cues; observers were not permitted to hear the deceivers speak, but merely observed their nonverbal behavior while they were communicating. Knapp, Hart and Dennis (1974) suggest that the discrepancy between verbal and nonverbal cues may provide the most useful information for detecting deceit. No data are available concerning how verbal cues interact with nonverbal cues emanating from the head only, body only, or head and body to provide jurors with information that will enhance the possibility of detecting deception. The present study sought data relative to these questions when observers are exposed either to color or black-and-white videotaped testimony.

More specifically, this study used Ekman and Friesen's (1974) deception-inducing technique while altering the questions asked of interviewees and using videotapes in a fashion more similar to the courtroom. The individuals interviewed were videotaped in both color and black-and-white with sound. Camera shots included a closeup of the head and a head and body shot. A body only videotape was created by blocking out the head on the videotape viewing screen; this shot was included for theoretical reasons and to reexamine Ekman and Friesen's findings. The interviewees were not only asked how they felt about the pleasant and unpleasant stimuli they were viewing, they were also questioned concerning the facts of an event which they viewed on videotape. This allowed us to identify any differences between lying about feelings (emotional testimony) and lying about observed events (factual testimony). Audiotape and transcripts were made of all interviews. Finally, observers were shown videotapes in all these conditions with or without sound. These variations yield a fourteen condition design. Twelve conditions were completely crossed: two (color, monochromatic) by three (head only, body only, head and body) by two (visual and audio, visual only). The audiotape and transcript conditions were not contained in the completely crossed design, but were compared with the color and monochromatic conditions.

## Procedures

### Creating Stimuli

Twenty-three criminal justice seniors (nineteen males and four females) at Michigan State University served as interviewees in this study. Each interviewee received a letter from the Director of the School of Criminal Justice encouraging participation in the study, which ostensibly sought to identify personal characteristics that contribute to success as a police officer.

Upon arriving, all students were told by an experimenter and a police inspector, who served as the interviewer, that police officers often have to mask their true feelings and/or lie. They were also told that the research aimed at developing a screening procedure to be used in hiring police officers, and that the School of Criminal Justice would receive information concerning the performance of its seniors on the test. This cover story sought to heighten interviewee ego-involvement in lying by stressing the favorable career consequences of successful falsehood.

Students were initially asked their name, address, major, and other demographic questions which were always answered truthfully. Their answers provided observers with a sample of truthful behavior upon which later veracity judgments could be based. This phase of the interview is similar to what transpires in a courtroom when witnesses take the stand. Usually, they are asked to state their names for the record and to respond to other demographic questions. Thus, actual jurors are provided with truthful responses for comparison with later testimony.

Prior to questioning, each student viewed a videotape of a man being sentenced for murder. They were questioned concerning the details of this videotape, and consistent with prior instructions, they answered some questions truthfully and others untruthfully. After questioning concerning the sentencing, the students viewed a series of pleasant slides depicting landscapes and unpleasant slides depicting burn victims and were asked to describe their feelings while viewing the slides. As in the Ekman and Friesen (1974) study, they were instructed to always lie while viewing the slides of burn victims and to always tell the truth while viewing the pleasant landscape slides.

All interviews were videotaped in color. Separate cameras were used to obtain close-ups of the interviewees' heads and the full head and body shots. The monochromatic stimulus was achieved by switching the videotape recorder to the black-and-white mode during presentation to the observers. The body only tape was created by using the full head and body shots and blocking the head from the view of the observers. To keep the audio quality constant across conditions, television monitors, with the video eliminated, were used in the audio only situations. Finally, the videotapes were transcribed for the transcription situation.

*Editing the Tapes*

Of the twenty-three interviewees, seven did not provide completed tapes, either because they failed to follow instructions (e.g., did not lie when instructed to do so) or because of equipment failure. One of these individuals was included as a practice trial to demonstrate the format of the tapes, but the rest were eliminated. Thus, observers viewed tapes composed of the sixteen successfully completed interviews.

Whatever the observable cues from which inferences of veracity are made, we can safely assume everyone does not emit them equally. Fay and Middleton (1941) found that their respondents were judged accurately by as few as 50.9% of the observers and by as many as 62.8%. Some of our student interviewees probably presented many cues perceived by observers as indicative of lying *both* while they were lying and telling the truth. If, by chance, only such a person's lying segment were selected for judgment, observers' accuracy scores would probably be spuriously inflated; not because they were able to discriminate between the interviewee's lying and truthful behavior, but because the interviewee always looked as if he or she were lying. Conversely, other persons may not give off many revealing cues; they may always look as if they are telling the truth. If only their truthful behavior appeared on a tape, accuracy scores would again be increased, not because of the observers' ability to detect veracity, but because of these individuals' truthful appearing behavior.

To minimize such biasing effects, two tapes were created; one the inverse of the other. Thus, if an interviewee's truthful segment were randomly selected for inclusion on one tape, his or her lying segment was included on the other. Both tapes were used in each condition, with one-half of the observers viewing each version. This approach sought to produce detection scores with higher ecological validity than would be likely if only a truthful or lying sample of each interviewee's behavior had been included, since cell means for accuracy in each of the fourteen conditions are based on observations of both lying and truthful responses for each of the sixteen interviewees.

The format for both tapes was identical. All interviewees were first shown truthfully answering the demographic questions. This segment was immediately followed by the interviewee's lying or truthful testimony. The first eight interviewees provided factual testimony and the last eight emotional. For each type, four interviewees lied and four told the truth. Since the factual segments were always shown first, an order effect, such as fatigue or learning, possibly could have influenced responses to the emotional segments. Nevertheless, any order effect would be a constant across all treatment conditions, and unless such an effect interacted in some way with the experimental manipulations, it would not influence the comparisons of interest: accuracy scores *within* the various factual and emotional conditions. The potential benefit of varying the order was thus judged to be outweighed by the problem of introducing additional procedural complexity to an already complex study design.

*Observers*

Because of unavailability of actual jurors, observers were 719 undergraduate students enrolled in introductory communication classes at Michigan State University and 193 adult residents from the Lansing area. Each class of students was randomly assigned to one of the experimental conditions. Because they were assigned by class, the sample sizes are not uniform for all fourteen conditions. Since the number of available Lansing residents was limited, they were randomly assigned to the four conditions most closely simulating the circumstances of actual jury trials: head only, head and body, color, and monochromatic, all four conditions using audio.

*Data Collection*

Observers recorded their veracity judgments on paper. An attached cover page detailed the circumstances under which the tape had been created and explained the presentation format for the various segments. Observers were told that it was very important to all of the interviewees to deceive the police officer who was interrogating them.

To minimize the possibility that observers would make an approximately equal number of lying and truthful judgments, they were told the particular tape they were viewing might contain mostly truthful segments, mostly lying segments, or about equal numbers of each. Observers were instructed to make each judgment independently of their others. They were also told there was no relationship between the length of a segment and whether the interviewee was lying or telling the truth, and that the same answer could be truthful for some interviewees and untruthful for others.

Observers were shown a practice segment to ensure that they understood the task. The experimenter then played the rest of the tape. Each of the sixteen interviewees were shown individually to the observers, who made their judgments about each presentation before continuing to the next interview. Each observer viewed one of the tapes in one of the fourteen conditions, with both tapes shown once in each of the conditions.

## Results

Each observer made sixteen judgments, eight based on interviewees responding to the factual content of the sentencing episode and eight based on interviewees reporting their feelings while viewing the two sets of slides. Accuracy scores for each observer were arrived at by separately adding the number of correct judgments within each segment and dividing by eight. Consequently, each observer's accuracy was represented by two proportions, one for the factual segment and one for the emotional segment. Scores have a possible range of 0 to 1.0, with .50 representing four correct judgments out of the eight attempted.

Table 7.1 presents the means for factual accuracy in all conditions. The three-way analysis of variance for the twelve conditions which fit within the factorial design revealed a significant main effect for shot ($F = 5.78$, $p < .05$). Inspection of the marginal means in Table 7.1 indicates that observers who viewed the body only ($M = .497$) were less accurate than both head

## TABLE 7.1
### Mean Accuracy Scores for Factual Testimony for Observers in the 14 Conditions*

| | Head Only | | Shot Body Only | | Head and Body | | |
| | Audio and Visual | Visual Only | Audio and Visual | Visual Only | Audio and Visual | Visual Only | Marginal Means |
|---|---|---|---|---|---|---|---|
| Color | .608 | .492 | .547 | .449 | .637 | .438 | .533 |
| Black and white | .578 | .468 | .560 | .433 | .583 | .492 | .519 |
| Marginal means | .593 | .480 | .553 | .441 | .610 | .480 | |
| | | .537 | | .497 | | . 5 4 5 | |

*Multiple $R^2$ = .13

| | | | Visual and audio = .585 |
| Transcript only | Audio only | | Visual only = .467 |
| .625 | .618 | | Grand mean = .540 |

## TABLE 7.2
### Mean Accuracy Scores for Emotional Testimony for Observers in the 14 Conditions*

| | Head Only | | Shot Body Only | | Head and Body | | |
| | Audio and Visual | Visual Only | Audio and Visual | Visual Only | Audio and Visual | Visual Only | Marginal Means |
|---|---|---|---|---|---|---|---|
| Color | .508 | .477 | .527 | .519 | .511 | .468 | .505 |
| Black and white | .481 | .433 | .496 | .537 | .495 | .497 | .490 |
| Marginal means | .494 | .455 | .511 | .528 | .503 | .491 | |
| | | .475 | | .520 | | . 4 9 7 | |

*Multiple $R^2$ = .07

| | | | Visual and audio = .503 |
| Transcript only | Audio only | | Visual only = .491 |
| .522 | .473 | | Grand mean = .501 |

only observers (M = .537, $t$ = 2.31, p<.05) and head and body observers (M = .545, $t$ = 2.80, p<.05).

Table 7.2 summarizes the means for emotional accuracy in all cells. The analysis of variance again yielded a significant main effect for shot (F = 4.35, p<.05), but in this case, observers who viewed the body only (M = .520) were significantly more accurate in judging emotional accuracy than their head only counterparts (M = .475, $t$ = 3.02, p<.05), but did not differ from head and body observers (M = .497, $t$ = 1.54, p>.05).

A significant visaudio main effect for factual accuracy was observed (F = 61.15, p<.05). Examination of the means in Table 7.1 indicates that for all six pairs of conditions, observers who were privy to both channels of information were more accurate than those who received visual information only (M, all audiovisual conditions = .585; M, all visual only conditions = .467). By contrast, no main effects were found for visaudio on emotional accuracy, nor did this variable enter into any interactions.

The analyses produced no significant main effects or interactions for color versus monochromatic on either factual or emotional accuracy: the presence or absence of color cues exerted no appreciable impact on the ability of observers to detect deceptive behavior. The likely validity of this null finding is reinforced by statistical and logical considerations. Although both the factual and emotional analyses produced main effects for other variables, the color versus monochromatic effect did not approach significance. Using a medium effect size ($n^2$ = .06), the results of a power analysis (Cohen, 1969) indicated that the power associated with all main effects exceeded .99; while the power associated with the various interactions ranged from .80 to .99. Consequently, from a statistical standpoint, the likelihood of Type 2 error is remote.

Furthermore, upon considering the findings for the transcript and audio only conditions, there are no logical grounds to expect a difference in detection accuracy between the color and monochromatic groups. The expectation of a difference rests on the assumption that nonverbal cues provide assistance in detecting deception, and that color provides a more complete inventory of these cues. Results for the transcript and audio only conditions in this study, as well as the earlier mentioned findings of Maier and Thurber (1968), cast serious doubt on this assumption: detecting deception is apparently not enhanced by the presence of nonverbal cues. Given the failure of these cues to improve accuracy, there is no compelling reason to expect color observers to fare better than observers who viewed the monochromatic presentations.

Observers in the transcript condition had a mean factual accuracy score of .625, which did not differ significantly from audio only observers (M = .618). Mean accuracy for visual only observers (M = .467) was significantly lower than the mean for audio only observers ($t$ = 5.24, p<.05). Audio only also resulted in higher observer accuracy than all three visual only levels of the shot variable. Both the head and body and the head only conditions had means of .480 ($t$ = 4.51 in both cases, p<.05) while the body only condition had a mean of .441 ($t$ = 5.67, p<.05). As a whole, these outcomes suggest that the oral responses of the interviewees provided better grounds for inferences about factual veracity than their nonverbal cues.

The mean visual and audio factual accuracy scores across all conditions (.585) are not significantly different from the audio only mean of .618 ($t$ = 1.14, p>.05). Within the visual and audio conditions, only the body only condition (M = .553) differed significantly from the audio only mean of .618 ($t$ = 2.12, p<.05). The similarity of these means suggests that adding the nonverbal behaviors to the verbal content of the responses did not affect observer ability to detect factual deception.

For emotional deception, the mean accuracy scores for the transcript and audio only conditions did not differ significantly (M, transcript = .522; M audio only = .473, $t$ = 1.71, p>.05). Moreover, the visual only mean accuracy for all six scores (.491) did not differ significantly from the audio only mean of .473. Within the visual only conditions, only the body only mean of .528 was significantly greater than the audio only mean ($t = 2.09$, p<.05).

For all six visual and audio cells, the mean emotional accuracy score was .503, a value that does not differ significantly from the audio only condition ($t = 1.22$, p>.05). All three levels of the shot variable within the visual and audio conditions also do not differ significantly from the audio only mean (M, head only = .494, $t = <1$; M, body only = .511, $t = 1.47$; M, head and body = .503, $t = 1.16$, p>.05 in all three instances).

Table 7.3 reports a comparison of the factual and the emotional accuracy scores for the student and resident samples. As stated earlier, the residents were assigned to the four conditions most closely simulating the circumstances facing jurors in an actual videotaped trial: head and body versus head only, and

**TABLE 7.3**
**Means and $t$ Tests Comparing Factual and Emotional Accuracy Scores of Student and Resident Observers**

|  |  | Head Only | | Head and Body | |
|  |  | Students | Residents | Students | Residents |
| --- | --- | --- | --- | --- | --- |
| Color | Factual | .608 | .643 | .645 | .589 |
|  |  | $t = 1.02$, df = 97 | | $t = 1.47$, df = 110 | |
|  | Emotional | .508 | .461 | .520 | .482 |
|  |  | $t = 1.42$, df = 97 | | $t = 1.29$, df = 111 | |
| Black and white | Factual | .578 | .565 | .582 | .578 |
|  |  | $t = <1$, df = 107 | | $t = <1$, df = 100 | |
|  | Emotional | .483 | .460 | .493 | .488 |
|  |  | $t = <1$, df = 106 | | $t = <1$, df = 100 | |

color versus monochromatic, with audio in all four conditions. Student accuracy scores are somewhat higher than those of residents for seven of the eight possible comparisons. Examination of the *t*-tests reveals, however, that none of the comparisons are significant at the .05 level, and four of the eight obtained *t*-values are less than one. These results indicate that the results for the student sample are not markedly different from those that would have been obtained had residents comprised the entire sample.

## Discussion

The outcomes for factual and emotional deception vary in terms of the best sources of information for evaluating veracity. For emotional testimony, body only observers were more accurate than those who based their judgments on the head only and head and body segments, a finding consistent with the earlier study of Ekman and Friesen (1974). For factual segments, however, a strong opposite trend was observed; head only and head and body observers had higher factual accuracy scores than body only observers.

This result pinpoints a possible shortcoming of Ekman and Friesen's (1969) viewpoint regarding the parts of the body most likely to reveal cues signaling deception. They argue that because the face has a greater information "sending capacity" than other parts of the body, people are most aware of their facial behavior, and consequently, can control it better than other bodily behaviors. Unfortunately, a procedural problem common to their study and our replication makes it hard to evaluate their position. Recall that the lying interviewees in both studies were always lying about their feelings when exposed to extremely stressful materials. The fact that the present study replicated Ekman and Friesen's results for emotional but not factual accuracy suggests that the cues from which lying was correctly inferred in the emotional segments may have resulted from the interviewee's exposure to these stressful materials *themselves* and not from false statements about her or his emotions. On the other hand, a more straightforward application of the Ekman and Friesen notion of the information "sending capacity" of parts of the body could account for the higher factual accuracy in the conditions where the faces were visible. Thus, Ekman and Freisen may be right in asserting that the face has the highest sending capacity for a wide range of message types, including nonverbal indicators of deception, but they may be overestimating the extent to which most people learn to control these nonverbal indicators. Further research is needed to resolve this issue.

The present results have several implications for courtroom trials. As far as the use of videotaped depositions and trials is concerned, the fact that observers exposed to color and monochromatic presentations were not differentially accurate in detecting deception suggests that use of less costly monochromatic taping systems poses no serious threat to juror ability to assess the veracity of witnesses. Furthermore, in terms of typical courtroom procedures, it is encouraging to note that the findings suggest the content of testimony contributes to, rather than detracting from detection accuracy, especially in the case of factual deception.

The most intriguing findings, however, stem from the generally low accuracy scores on the part of all observers, a result consistent with previous research. The highest accuracy (.625) occurred for jurors who read the transcripts of factual testimony, and only this situation produced a mean accuracy score much higher than the .50 score indicative of chance accuracy. These results support our skepticism about juror ability to detect deception on the part of unfamiliar witnesses and suggest room for caution in assessing whether jurors can perform this traditional function effectively.

## EFFECTS OF PRESENTATIONAL MODE ON DETECTING DECEPTION: AN EXTENDED REPLICATION

Although the previous study permitted comparison of the influence of four mediated modes of presentation on observer ability to detect deceptive communication, it did not include a live condition. Since the live setting is the accepted courtroom standard for comparison, and since many legal experts believe it provides optimal opportunity for jurors to assess the veracity of witnesses, our second study incorporated a live condition into the design.

Also, the second study used procedures calculated to engender more ego-involvement on the part of persons presenting deceptive testimony. Most students of deception believe that high ego-involvement is needed to stimulate nonverbal cues which signal deception; if there is little motivation and risk associated with lying, individuals should be able to lie more convincingly. Though ego-involvement seemed high in the first study, we believed the deception-inducing procedure used in the second study would further heighten involvement, thus approximating more closely the situation that exists when witnesses perjure themselves.

Because most of the criminal justice majors who presented deceptive messages in the first study were male, we were unable to control the sexual composiion of the interviewee/observer dyads. Since prior research has shown that this factor can affect accuracy of detection (Fay and Middleton, 1941; Maier, 1965; Mehrabian, 1969, 1971; Shulman, 1973), we equalized the sexual composition of the dyads in the second study.

Finally, the present study examined the relative plausibility of three hypotheses regarding the relationship of available information to accuracy of detecting deception. All three hypotheses posit a relationship between the two variables, even though the assumed relationships differ and rest on different mediating processes. Thus, two possibilities existed: first, if some relationship were observed, it would be possible to argue that one hypothesis is more tenable than the others; second, if no relationship were to emerge, all three hypotheses would fail to receive support.

## Available Information and Judgmental Accuracy: Three Hypotheses

The *information utilization* hypothesis suggests that as the amount of verbal and nonverbal information available to observers increases, their accuracy in detecting deception should also increase. The rationale underlying this explanation holds that, to the extent that the "richness" of available cues is directly related to increased perceptual acuity in deceptive transactions, observers should be more capable of detecting signals of deceit, and subsequently, be able to judge the veracity of information presented by a communicator more accurately. Researchers involved with the study of teleconferencing (Ryan, 1976) have invoked this rationale, and it is at least implied by Ekman and Friesen (1969, 1974) in their discussion of nonverbal leakage and clues to deception. They suggest that if an observer not only sees behaviors originating in areas of the body having a relatively high sending capacity — e.g., the face and voice — but also cues generated from areas having lower sending capacity — e.g., the hands, legs, and feet — the additional information provided by the latter cues should facilitate detection of deception by increasing signals of its occurrence. However, Ekman and Friesen (1974) only compared the accuracy of judgments of observers who viewed the deceiver's head only with those who viewed the body only, thus not directly testing the information utilization hypothesis.

Our first study compared accuracy scores over a wider range of conditions, with observers viewing both factual and emotional testimony. Recall that observers who viewed factual testimony had lower accuracy scores (49.7%) when viewing the body only than when viewing factual testimony in the head only condition (53.7%) and head and body condition (54.5%). When observers heard testimony concerning the emotional state of the interviewees, those in the body only condition had higher accuracy scores (52%) than observers in either the head and body (49.7%) or the head only (47.5%) conditions. Disregarding the not highly generalizable body only condition, the between-camera shot findings of the previous study seem to support the knowledge utilization hypothesis. However, additional findings of highest accuracy among observers experiencing factual testimony in the audio only (61.8%) and transcript (62.5%) conditions contradict the hypothesis and point to a need for more careful examination of the process surrounding the truth/deception attribution.

A second possible explanation, the *distraction* hypothesis, stems from research investigating the effects of distractive stimuli on persuasion and source credibility ratings, some of which was mentioned in the editing methods study in Chapter 5. It has been argued that distractions facilitate persuasion and perceived source credibility by dividing the attention of persuadees, reducing their ability to scrutinize incoming information and thus increasing their susceptibility to influence (Breitrose, 1966; Dorris, 1967; Osterhouse and Brock, 1970; Keating and Brock, 1974; Brandt, 1976).

The preceding reasoning may be appropriated to explain some experimental findings regarding deception (Maier and Thurber, 1968; first study of this chapter). To the extent that a deceiver attempts to convince others that his or her deceptive performance represents "normal" communication behavior, persuasive and deceptive settings are analogous. Increasing the amount of available verbal and nonverbal cues places greater demands on observer attention, perhaps reducing the ability to scrutinize specific behaviors. If so, then behavioral cues which are extraneous to truth/deception judgments — i.e., do not signal the occurrence of deception — may divert attention from cues which are potential indicators of deception, resulting in reduced accuracy in deception detection. Maier and Thurber (1968) have invoked a distraction effect as a possible explanation for their findings, and at this stage of research, the distraction hypothesis seems worthy of consideration.

A third alternative is the *information overload* hypothesis. This hypothesis predicts results similar to those predicted by the distraction hypothesis, but with a key difference. The distraction hypothesis posits that since receivers must attend to increasing amounts of information, their accuracy in detecting deception is reduced because they are utilizing extraneous as well as relevant cues, resulting in inhibition of the ability to scrutinize the latter. The information overload hypothesis, on the other hand, suggests that receivers are *blocking out* important cues. Danowski (1974) explains that when individuals receive more information than they can process simultaneously, they experience confusion which results in higher output of error. With respect to deceptive transactions, as visual and paralinguistic cues increase the total amount of information observers must process, some of them may reach an information processing ceiling and additional input may produce overload. As indicated earlier, *filtering* and *chunking* (Danowski, 1974) are two processing strategies observers can use to adapt to overload: both rely on stereotypic cognitive referents to avoid processing all the available information in a given setting. Perhaps stereotypes of deceivers are utilized in attempting to make judgments of veracity. If such stereotypes are inaccurate, as some research suggests (Exline et al., 1970), inaccurate judgments of truth or lying could be expected. Thus, the information overload hypothesis predicts that the greater the overload on an individual observer, as a function of increased available information from a broad spectrum sensory channel, the stronger the influence of inaccurate stereotypes on deception judgments, and presumably, the lower the accuracy of such judgments.

It is difficult to determine, a priori, which of these hypotheses is most accurate, and/or under what conditions. However, by varying the channel through which observers view truthful and deceitful communicators, obtaining estimates of the amount of verbal and nonverbal information afforded by each channel, and examining judgmental accuracy in relation to these variations, some insight may be gained. The present study attempts to explore this issue. As noted above, it also employs a live condition, along with video, audio, and transcript conditions, to determine their impact on the ability of observers to detect deception, a set of comparisons that should provide additional information about the functioning of these various modes of presentation in the courtroom.

## Procedures

### Interviewees

The interviewees wee six male and six female undergraduate students enrolled at Michigan State University who volunteered to participate in a study of "group problem-solving." Half were randomly assigned to a deception condition and half to a truthful condition. Each interviewee worked in a dyad with a confederate, whose status was not revealed until after the study was completed.

### Deception-Inducing Procedure

The procedure for inducing deception was modeled after one employed in previous research by Exline et al. (1970) and Shulman (1973). Interviewees were told that four-, three-, and two-person groups, as well as individuals, were being asked to engage in the same task (estimating the number of dots on a series of cards), to examine how group problem-solving strategies related to group size. They were told that since a governmental agency was providing funds for the project, and in order to motivate interest in the task, the group in each size category with the best performance would receive $50 to divide among its members. All interviewees were told they had been randomly assigned to a two-person group and matched with a student from another class (actually, the confederate).

Prior to the interviewee's arrival, the confederate randomly assigned him or her to either a truthful or deceptive condition; a cheating-implication procedure only was used for interviewees assigned to the latter condition. In all instances, the experimenter remained "blind" to the condition to avoid differential treatment of interviewees during the postprocedure interview. As indicated earlier, the assignment procedure controlled for sex, so that an equal number of males and females appeared in both lying and truthful conditions. The sex of observers was also controlled so that there were equal numbers of male-male, male-female, female-male, and female-female interviewee/observer dyads in each condition. Since Shulman (1973) found no effects from changing the sex of the confederate in this procedure, the same female confederate was used throughout the study.

The task required the dyad jointly to estimate the number of dots on a series of nine cards which the experimenter flashed in front of them for fifteen seconds. After viewing each card, the interviewee and confederate were told to confer as long as necessary to come up with one estimate for the number of dots.

At the beginning of each problem-solving session, a practice sample was presented. Then, before starting the actual problems, the experimenter mentioned that after each series of three cards she would provide the group with feedback concerning its progress by informing it of the correct answers for the completed cards. After the third card the confederate always requested this feedback, while the experimenter delayed giving it for "a couple of more trials, since you are taking so much time to decide." Between the fourth and sixth card, a second experimenter, who had been listening to the interaction via an intercom, interrupted the session to inform the first experimenter that she had an "important telephone call from the director of the research project." The first experimenter left the room to "take" the alleged call.

If the interviewee were in the truthful condition, the confederate simply engaged him or her in normal conversation during the experimenter's absence. However, if the interviewee were in the deception condition, the confederate went through a procedure to implicate him or her in the act of cheating.

The confederate observed the folder which the experimenter had left on her chair and wondered aloud if it contained the correct answers; she complained that the experimenter had "failed to supply promised feedback" and that "she could really use the $50." Next, the confederate suggested looking in the folder and, regardless of the interviewee's reaction, got up and began to leaf through it. Many interviewees helped the confederate, but regardless of their reaction, she read the correct answers aloud, identifying them as such, and jotted them down on a piece of scratch paper provided by the experimenter.

Since it was important that the first experimenter not know if the interviewee was assigned to a lying or a truthful condition, and to ensure that she would not return until the confederate had sufficient time to enact the procedure, a second experimenter listened from the observation room to the conversation between the confederate and the source. After the confederate had implicated the interviewee in cheating, the second experimenter told the first experimenter she could return from the alleged telephone call. The duration of the first experimenter's absence was held constant for all interviewees, regardless of condition, to avoid cueing the experimenter as to the type of condition. The timing also protected the confederate's cover since the intevieweehad little time to question the confederate before the first experimenter returned. The task was then completed, with the confederate always using the dishonestly obtained scores to make accurate estimates. In this way, unless the interviewee reported the confederate to the experimenter (and none did) he or she was implicated in cheating.

## Interviewing for Messages

After the task was completed, the experimenter took the dyad into another room to interview them concerning the strategies they used to arrive at answers to the task. The experimenter always began by interviewing the interviewee first, under the pretense that the confederate would be interviewed next.

The first five questions of the interview provided observers with a sample of the interviewee's truthful behavior, as well as providing demographic information for future analysis. The next six questions dealt with the strategies used to perform the task. If the interviewee was in the implication procedure, the remainder of his or her answers were untruthful, since no interviewee mentioned that cheating had occurred.

During the interview, observers viewed the interviewee through a one-way mirror. In addition, videotapes, audiotapes, and transcripts were constructed from a videotape shot from the same angle as the live observation and through the same one-way mirror. Besides controlling for sex of interviewee/observer pairs, interviewees and observers were strangers.

Following the postprocedure interview all interviewees were debriefed and given detailed explanations of the study.

## Observers

Eighty undergraduate students enrolled at Michigan State University participated as observers. Because the present study included a live condition, a rather serious procedural problem had to be overcome. The time required for briefing, participation, and debriefing of each interviewee amounted to approximately one hour. Given twelve interviewees, this would have required observers in the live condition to attend a twelve-hour experimental sessions, which, because of fatigue and its potential contaminating effects, was deemed impractical. On the other hand, the time actually needed to observe and judge the veracity of interviewees was only about ten to fifteen minutes. Thus, in the video, audio, and transcript conditions, observers would need only ten to fifteen minutes per interviewee. To minimize the time required and still ensure that they judged all twelve interviewees, observers were counterbalanced across conditions and interviewees using a simple Latin square design (Lindquist, 1953). Thus, all observers were required to observe three interviewees in each of the four conditions.

After the experimenter explained the implication procedure to all observers, they saw, heard, or read the interviews of three interviewees in each condition, and made a judgment as to whether or not the interviewee was lying or telling the truth. As indicated, the live condition observations were made through a one-way mirror; during the task and implication procedure the observers remained in a separate conference room with no visual or audible access to the interviewees.

## Development of Information Measures

To obtain measures for testing the three alternative hypotheses, eight trained coders provided holistic estimates of nonverbal and total available information, with estimates based on the following definitions:

> Nonverbal information refers to the amount of information available from nonverbal behaviors such as facial expression, eye contact, nodding, hand and body movement, posture, pausing, "ums" and "ahs," and anything beyond actual words. Nonverbal information refers to *how* people communicate, *not* what they say.
>
> Total information is a holistic estimate of all available information provided by a stimulus. It is the kind of judgment you would make if I asked you which of two books or movies provided you with the most information.

Coders were cautioned that information is not necessarily the sum of verbal and nonverbal information. Redundancy in nonverbal and verbal cues may produce a lower figure for total information than the sum of nonverbal and verbal information (Wiener and Mehrabian, 1968). For this reason, it was emphasized that the estimates should be made independently, even though the variables are not theoretically independent. Intercoder reliability estimates were computed for nonverbal information, total information, the ratio of nonverbal to total information, and the logarithmic transformations of nonverbal and total information estimates (Cronbach, 1951). Alpha coefficients were .98, .96, .99, .99, and .98 respectively (p $<$ .05).

Coders were trained to make ratio-level judgments of nonverbal and total information using direct interval estimation:

> The standard for direct interval estimation consists of two stimuli possessing different amounts of the attribute being rated. Each is assigned a number of points, e.g., 100 and 200. The one with the smallest amount of the attribute is assigned the lowest

number of points. The point assignments to the two stimuli should be approximately equal to the ratio of the amounts of the attributes they possess [Silverman and Johnston, 1975: 464].

This standard interval thus serves as a psychological "ruler" upon which estimates are based.

Two samples from the first study were used as the standard interval for coder estimation. These samples were chosen from the original sixteen interviews based on reported pretest values obtained from fifteen undergraduates concerning available nonverbal, verbal, and total information for each segment. Two segments were selected; the mean of the first was approximately one-half the mean of the second for both nonverbal and total information, based on pretest data. Accordingly, the first segment was assigned values of 100 and 150 for nonverbal and total information, respectively, while the second segment was assigned values of 200 and 300 for nonverbal and total information, respectively. Coders then provided estimates of available nonverbal and total information for all interviewees via all four transmission channels.

## Results

Earlier it was suggested that the availability of information, particularly nonverbal information, as a function of variations in the communication channel may affect differences in the accuracy of attributions of veracity made by observers. Thus, a model in which judgmental accuracy is the dependent variable, perceived available total and nonverbal information are intermediate endogenous variables, and the various channels are exogenous is appropriate. Accordingly, this model was estimated using a two-stage least squares procedure (Namboodiri et al., 1975). The basic model appears in Figure 7.1.

In addition, analysis of variance of judgmental accuracy by condition and *a posteriori* comparison of cell means utilizing the Newman-Keuls procedure were conducted. This provided a second means of examining experimental main effects, as well as facilitating simplicity of presentation.

# FIGURE 7.1: A MODEL OF THE RELATION BETWEEN AC-CURACY, AVAILABLE INFORMATION, AND CHANNEL

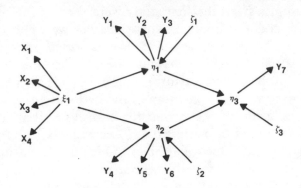

Where: $\xi_1$ = Communication Channel (True Variable)
$\eta_1$ = Available Nonverbal Information (True Variable)
$\eta_2$ = Available Total Information (True Variable)
$\eta_3$ = Ability to Attribute Truth or Deception (True Variable)
$\zeta_1$ = Disturbance Term for $\eta_1$
$\zeta_2$ = Disturbance Term for $\eta_2$
$\zeta_3$ = Disturbance Term for $\eta_3$
$X_1$ = Live Condition (Indicator of $\xi_1$)
$X_2$ = Video Condition (Indicator of $\xi_1$)
$X_3$ = Audio Condition (Indicator of $\xi_1$)
$X_4$ = Transcript Condition (Indicator of $\xi_1$)
$Y_1$ = First Coder's Estimate of $\eta_1$
$Y_2$ = Second Coder's Estimate of $\eta_1$
$Y_3$ = Third Coder's Estimate of $\eta_1$
$Y_4$ = First Coder's Estimate of $\eta_2$
$Y_5$ = Second Coder's Estimate of $\eta_2$
$Y_6$ = Third Coder's Estimate of $\eta_2$
$Y_7$ = Observer Judgmental Accuracy

*Channel Variation and Perceived Information Availability*

The first stage of the two-stage least squares procedure (2SLS) consists of ordinary least squares regression. In this case, two separate equations had to be estimated; the first to determine the path coefficients between perceived nonverbal information and the exogenous variables, and the second to determine the paths between perceived available total information and the exogenous, as well as nonverbal information variables.

It was assumed that variations in the communication channel would result in covariation in coder perceptions of the amount of available nonverbal information. The results strongly support this assumption, with variations in the channel accounting for greater than 99% of the variance in perceived available nonverbal information. These results also serve as an indirect check of the success of the procedure for manipulating available information in terms of communication channel. (Note: for purposes of clarity of presentation, details of the 2SLS analyses are minimized. The interested reader can find these details, including the tables for the equations, in Miller et al., forthcoming).

It was also assumed that channel variations, as well as perceived available nonverbal information, would result in variations in coder perceptions of available total information. Again, the results are strongly supportive ($R^2 = .969$), and also serve as an indirect check of the procedure for controlling the availability of information, a crucial variable in the present study.

*Information Availability and Judgmental Accuracy*

The results pertaining to channel variation and perceived information availability are fairly straightforward and not particularly surprising. Of more importance are the findings pertaining to information availability as a predictor of accurate judgments of veracity. By using the two-stage least squares procedure, the endogenous variables in the structural model could be "purified" in such a way that their correlations with disturbance terms were eliminated. Thus, given minimal measurement and/or sampling error, a fairly accurate estimate of the relation between information availability and observer accuracy was possible.

The results of this analysis suggest that variations in availability of information, as a function of communication channel, do not predict judgmental accuracy very well. The multiple R was only .064, accounting for less than 1% of the variance in accuracy scores.

## Channel Variation and Judgmental Accuracy

A major aim of the present study was to examine the ability of observers to make accurate attributions of veracity under live, video, audio, and transcript conditions. Although the results of the two-stage least squares regression obviously take such variations in communication channel into account, it is not clear how each affects judgmental accuracy, based on examination of these results alone. A simple analysis of variance of accuracy scores was computed to shed further light on this issue. While the analysis yielded a significant F of 2.61 (p <.05), the only significant two condition comparison involved the live and audiotape condition, with observers in the former condition being more accurate in detecting deception.

## Discussion

Findings of the second study do not support any of the three hypotheses: information utilization, information overload, or distraction. In fact, the multiple R of .064 indicates that available total information accounts for less than 1% of the variance in accuracy scores. The relatively high accuracy in the transcript condition (46.7%) rules out any linear relationship between available nonverbal and/or total information and the ability of untrained observers to detect deception on the part of strangers. The comparatively high accuracy observed in the transcript condition, an outcome congruent with the first study, also suggests that an attribute of that channel, distinct from type and amount of information, may provide an explanation. Amount of time an observer has to examine the message and the ability of an observer to reexamine the message are two such qualities of transcripts worthy of additional inquiry.

Considering the low accuracy scores obtained in all conditions — 56.7% for the live, 46.7% for videotape and transcript, and 31.6% for the audio — it is highly questionable whether untrained observers can accurately detect deception on the part of strangers, the task faced by jurors when attempting to assess the veracity of witnesses. None of the mean accuracy scores differed significantly from the 50% criterion researchers have defined as chance accuracy in prior studies. Of course, this criterion is somewhat arbitrary in the sense that people generally do not expect others to be lying 50% of the time. In the present study, however, half the responses were truthful and half untruthful, thus making the 50% figure appropriate.

A few studies (Maier and Thurber, 1968; Ekman and Friesen, 1974; first study of this chapter) have obtained accuracy scores significantly above the 50% criterion. Still, the deception-inducing procedures employed in these studies can be criticized for problems which may inflate accuracy scores. Maier and Thurber (1968) had students "role-play" deceivers. When role-playing, lying behavior is not inconsistent with matters of known fact, i.e., deceivers act as they *believe* someone who is lying acts. Not only is the tendency to emphasize "lying" behaviors, the role player has no real motivation to succeed in the performance. Thus, such a technique, at worst, inflates the accuracy scores of observers, while at best it has been seriously questioned as a research technique, since no one seems to know whether role players know how real liars behave (Freedman, 1969).

In both the Ekman and Friesen (1974) study and the first study reported here, individuals always lied while observing an unpleasant stimulus and told the truth while viewing a pleasant stimulus. This procedure systematically increased the cues of discomfort and arousal coming from the group of liars. Such cues of arousal would be interpreted by observers as resulting from lying rather than other extraneous factors, since that was the explanation offered by the social context in which observers made their judgments (Schachter and Singer, 1962). The arousal cues stemming from the unpleasant stimulus would thus have made it easier for observers to identify liars.

The deception-inducing procedure used in this study was chosen to overcome some of the criticisms of past deception-inducing techniques. We realized that a more generalizable deception-inducing procedure might produce lower accuracy scores than role-playing or lying about emotional responses to unpleasant stimuli; indeed, the resultant accuracy scores (56.7%, 46.7%, 46.7%, 31.6%) were lower, but we believe more generalizable than past scores. Given the criticism of past deception-inducing techniques, the generally low scores found when using these past techniques, and the low scores found in the present study, the claim that untrained observers can accurately detect deception on the part of relative strangers is highly questionable.

Apparently, the use of videotape to present testimony of witnesses does not exert any marked impact on the accuracy of juror judgments of witness veracity. Although the percentage of accurate judgments was highest in the live setting, it was not significantly greater than the percentage of accurate judgments in the videotape condition. Consequently, a decision on using videotape to present the testimony of witnesses need not hinge upon this communication medium's deleterious effect upon juror ability to assess the veracity of witnesses.

One important limitation of this study deserves mention. In the transcript condition, observers read the written transcript rather than having it read to them. This procedure, of course, deviates from the normal courtroom practice of reading the transcript to the jurors and into the record. In actual trials, the interrogating attorney will often select a colleague from his own law firm to read the witness's responses. Such a procedure raises the possibility of introducing bias into the proceedings by coloring, intentionally or unintentionally, the witness's responses by use of paralinguistic and nonverbal cues. If the communication style of the individual selected to read the absent witness's testimony from the transcript affects juror perceptions of the absent witness, an argument would materialize suggesting the use of an alternative mode of presentation. For this reason, we made the decision to allow the observers to read the transcript in this study.

## SUMMING UP

This chapter has reported the results of two studies dealing with the possible influence of mode of presentation and type of witness camera shot on the ability of jurors to detect deceptive testimony. The outcomes of the first study revealed that head only and head and body shots resulted in greater accuracy in detecting factual deception than did a body only shot. Conversely, emotional accuracy was greatest for the body only shot, though we suggested that this difference may have resulted from a procedural shortcoming.

Taken together, the two studies indicated that accuracy in detecting deception was not significantly affected by the mode of presenting testimony; in fact, we stressed that high levels of nonverbal information may actually hamper attempts to assess witness veracity. By far the most interesting result was the relatively low level of accuracy across all presentation modes, a finding which suggests that jurors are probably not notably effective in determining whether a witness is testifying truthfully.

## 8

## A FINAL SUMMATION

From the outset, our research has centered on a single objective: to provide research findings bearing upon one issue relating to the possible use of videotape in courtroom trials. As we stressed in Chapter 1, policy decisions regarding the introduction of this technology into the legal system hinge on numerous complex legal, social, and behavioral issues. Hence, we prefer to be both relatively brief and reasonably cautious in drawing conclusions. Although the question of whether jurors respond differently to videotaped trial presentations than to live ones is an important one, we realize that many other considerations also affect the extent to which videotape becomes a more prominent part of the courtroom communication milieu.

### LOOKING BACK

Having underscored our cautious posture, we offer the following as our most general conclusion. *Within the procedural confines of our research, there is no evidence to suggest that the use of videotape exerts any deleterious effects on the juror responses studied; in fact, as far as retention of trial-related information is concerned, it appears that videotaped testimony sometimes results in higher retention levels.* Given this assertion, we shall temper it immediately by reviewing some of the limitations (or the "procedural confines") that should be considered when evaluating it.

First, our research has focused almost entirely on matters commonly dealt with in civil trials. We reached this decision consciously, since the most extensive use of videotape, at least until this time, has been in the civil area. Whether similar results would be obtained in criminal trials remains uncertain, though we are unaware of any radical differences in jury box makeup that should drastically alter our civil trial outcomes.

Second, all of the studies described have dealt with simulated or reenacted trials, trial segments, or depositions, rather than actual trials. Having noted this fact, we hasten to add that in several of the studies jurors were led to believe they were participating in actual trials, and the available evidence indicates that they accepted the veracity of the presiding judge's remarks. Nevertheless, we also conducted some studies where participants were aware that they were role-playing jurors, and we have already expressed a healthy skepticism about the ecological validity of this role-playing approach.

We strove to avoid using students in those studies whose ecological validity and generalizability would be adversely affected. Obviously, this was not always possible; however, many of the studies shared overlapping foci, and to some degree represented modified replications. Consistent findings across these studies increased our confidence in the conclusions. Our studies, broadly speaking, can be clustered into four different groups focusing upon: differences in mode of presentation of trial-related material, the effects of inadmissible materials upon juror behavior, the ability of jurors to detect deceptive testimony across different modes of presentation, and the effects of several video production techniques on juror response. As demonstrated in Chapter 2, none of our conclusions relating to any one of these four clusters is solely dependent upon findings derived from student samples.

Third, even within the realm of civil litigation, we have sampled from relatively few types of cases and over relatively few time periods of trial activity — i.e., less than an hour of testimony through a three and one-half hour trial. Again, as with the issue of using civil cases entirely, the importance of these limited samples is directly related to the number of commonsense arguments that can be constructed concerning the likelihood that other types of case content or other trial lengths might yield different outcomes. Regarding the former, we have been unable to think of any compelling reasons why a change in case content — e.g., going from an automobile injury case to a slip-and-fall case — would be likely to alter drastically the findings of our studies. On the other hand, trial length could affect the differences in juror retention of trial-related information that were observed between live and videotaped presentations of testimony. As mentioned in Chapter 4, while videotaped testimony may generate greater juror interest — and consequently, greater retention of trial-related information — for the relatively short time periods studied, this potential advantage of the videotape medium might be dissipated in a lengthy trial. Note that we do not necessarily believe this would be the case, but we are aware that such an argument could reasonably be advanced.

Finally, several of our studies have yielded no significant differences in juror responses to live and videotaped trial materials. From an applied perspective, this lack of differences creates no problems since it suggests that the two presentation media are comparable. Unfortunately, it does pose some interpretative difficulties, since the logic of the statistical model underlying the research prevents us from attaching a precise level of significance (or confidence) to our findings of no differences. Stated differently, failure to reject the statistical null hypothesis — in this case, failure to detect significant differences between juror responses to live and videotaped trial materials — may signal a true absence of differences between the two presentational modes or it may represent an instance of

Type 2 error. Since the likelihood of Type 2 error is affected by numerous considerations (sample size, measurement error, etc.), we can only assess the probable validity of no difference findings by reporting power analyses where appropriate and by considering the adequacy of our research procedures as they relate to these various sources of possible error.

In one or two instances, we concede that procedural difficulties contributed to the high likelihood of Type 2 error. For example, in the first study dealing with deletion of inadmissible materials, a number of jurors originally scheduled to participate in the research were called away to serve in actual trials, and as a consequence, the sample size available for the various trial conditions was severely depleted. This juror attrition undoubtedly sharply decreased the power of our tests to detect differences in juror responses to the varying amounts of inadmissible materials used in the trial.

In most cases, however, we feel we have minimized those factors likely to produce Type 2 error. For the majority of the studies, sample size has been robust, the research has been conducted in realistic settings, and the instruments used to measure juror response have been carefully pretested and refined. All of these considerations, as well as the results of the power analyses, point toward a reasonably powerful test of the null hypothesis; and we are quite confident that, in most cases, our failure to reject the null results from a lack of systematic differences in juror responses to alternative modes of presentation. Beyond this assertion, the logic of the statistical model itself precludes further evaluation.

To a large extent, one's assessment of the relative importance of the research described here hinges on his or her views concerning two issues. The first involves the nature of the trial itself. Our research has been grounded in the assumption that a trial is a rule-governed, information-processing event and that juror decision-making should be influenced primarily by the facts and evidence of the case. Given this assumption, it makes good sense to worry about the possible effects of the videotape

medium on such juror behaviors as retention of trial-related information and actual verdicts and awards. On the other hand,
alternative assumptions about the nature of the trial process are
certainly defensible, and if one accepts an alternative assumption, other research priorities may be implied. For example, we
mentioned in Chapter 1 that some scholars conceive of a trial as
a ritualistic or dramatistic rite: the trial serves the function of
satisfying society's need for an institution that permits orderly,
nonviolent resolution of disputes. Acceptance of this viewpoint
implies a different ordering of research priorities; specifically,
questions concerning the extent to which the use of videotaped
trial materials adds to or detracts from the dramatic impact of
the trial and the subsequent perceptions of a just system for
resolving conflicts would receive primary attention. We grant
that our decisions to pursue certain questions and hypotheses
rather than others rest on our particular view of the nature and
function of the trial process.

At an even more basic level, one's assessment of the relative
significance of our findings depends on his or her response to a
fundamental epistemological question: what kinds of evidence
constitute the best grounds for making assertions about the probable effects of videotaped trial materials on juror response?
Obviously and not surprisingly, we subscribe to the empiricist
tenet that systematically assembled observations, drawn from
representative samples of juror respondents, provide the
soundest grounds for making inferences about the courtroom
effects of videotape. Thus, while the findings of these studies
stop short of establishing definitive answers to the numerous
questions raised, they provide an improved climate for drawing
inferences, since some data are better than no data at all.

## LOOKING AT THE PRESENT

The following general conclusions are supported by our
research:

(1) The use of videotape in the courtroom does not significantly
affect juror verdicts.

(2) The use of videotape in the courtroom does not significantly affect the monetary awards to plaintiffs made by jurors.

(3) The use of videotape significantly affects the amount of trial-related information retained by jurors during a trial, with jurors retaining more information from taped testimony, particularly when it is presented monochromatically.

(4) Juror perceptions of attorney credibility can be significantly influenced by different editing and production techniques that are a part of available video technology.

(5) Juror perceptions of witness credibility are affected by the use of videotape in the courtroom.

(6) Videotaped presentations of different types of witnesses (strong and weak) affect juror evaluations of the credibility of the witness.

(7) The use of videotape in the courtroom to present witness testimony does not significantly affect juror judgments of the veracity of the testimony presented.

(8) The deletion of inadmissible materials from testimony does not appear to exert a strong impact on juror perceptions of attorney credibility. It does appear, however, that jurors do ignore instructions to disregard inadmissible materials (a sort of double disregard effect) to the extent that the materials are frequently brought up during deliberations.

(9) Within the province of the simple production techniques studied in this research, characteristics of the witness appear to exert more impact on juror response than do production decisions. Stated differently, the presentation skills of the witness are more important than variations in such factors as a number of cameras and types of shots *given* the relatively rudimentary techniques studied.

Within the confines of juror responses examined in these studies, no evidence suggests that videotaped trials, when compared to their live counterparts, exercise a negative impact on the juror decision-making process. Compared to live trial jurors, those jurors who viewed a videotaped trial reported similar verdicts, had comparable perceptions of trial participants, retained at least as much trial-related information, and expressed similar levels of interest and motivation.

The research dealing with retention of trial-related information following live, black-and-white, and color videotape presentations of testimony indicated that while jurors retain significantly less trial-related information in all three modes over time, more rapid decay occurs in the live presentation. Additionally, jurors retain more central arguments and facts when exposed to monochromatic testimony than its more expensive color counterpart.

Findings from the study concerning the effects of introducing videotaped segments of witness testimony into an otherwise live trial indicated that certain witness characteristics influence juror perceptions of trial participants differently, depending upon whether the live or videotape medium is used to present testimony. Thus, the unidimensional use of either medium will not have a uniform effect upon juror response to all witnesses and attorneys. Additional research is needed to identify the specific source characteristics that interact with the mode of presentation to produce these diverse effects.

Regarding the use of videotape to delete inadmissible materials from trial proceedings, the research reported here reveals no significant impact on juror response caused by either the inclusion or deletion of inadmissible materials, save for the fact that jurors do frequently bring up the information during their deliberations. Since other studies have reported verdict influences and since our own research reveals a tendency to introduce the information, it strikes us as judicially prudent to delete the inadmissible materials if possible. Videotape, of course, permits such deletion.

Two important implications accrue from the research dealing with various editing methods used to delete inadmissible materials. First, the process of editing per se appears to reduce the perceived credibility of trial participants. Second, since an inverse relationship exists between distraction and perceived credibility — i.e., the more distraction introduced by a given editing method, the less the perceived credibility of the participants — the most effective method for use in the courtroom is one producing the least distraction, in this case, the clean edit.

The research conducted thus far indicates that the videotape medium does not significantly reduce juror ability to detect deceptive testimony, particularly when the testifying individual appears alone on video monitors. For use in the courtroom, the findings suggest a camera view which includes the entire head and body of the witness to maximize accurate assessment of both factual and emotional testimony. Videotaping in the more expensive color mode does not appear to aid the juror in detecting deception. Still, the relatively low accuracy levels observed in live, video, audio, and transcript presentations raise serious issues about the ability of jurors to detect false testimony regardless of the mode of communication in which it is presented. The visual element in videotaped presentations appears to add little to the accuracy of veracity judgments; indeed, people who read written transcripts were consistently as accurate or more accuarate in detecting deception.

While some interaction between individual characteristics — i.e., physical attractiveness and nonverbal communication effectiveness — and the mode of presentation may occur, preliminary findings suggest that video production techniques do not exert dramatic effects on juror perceptions of trial participants, nor the ultimate outcome of civil litigation. It should be emphasized, however, that research thus far has focused on relatively simple techniques. Moreover, since the problem is complex, the most prudent initial strategy probably lies in rules for uniform courtroom use of videotape which stipulate fixed cameras. By keeping presentational formats constant for all trial participants, questions about the influence of "editorial" judgments and the possible inequities resulting from wealthier participants retaining professional videotaping advice can be circumvented.

Finally, the color format apparently enhances the credibility of witnesses, particularly those with strong communication skills. To the extent that a color presentation heightens this effect, it may place a greater premium on variables that are not congruent with legal norms concerning the trial decision-making process; i.e., the color format may magnify the importance of *image* at the expense of *information*.

## LOOKING FORWARD

Although our research has been relatively comprehensive, there remain numerous unexplored areas concerning videotape usage in the courtroom. In this concluding section, we deem it useful to discuss briefly a few areas that merit additional attention. Most of the research that will be suggested derives from issues raised by our own studies.

Our research examining the relationship between alternative modes of presentation and juror retention of trial-related information indicated that monochromatic videotape may enhance retention. However, the length of the trials and depositions used in these studies was relatively short. As noted earlier, whether or not this relationship holds for a wider range of trial time periods remains to be determined by future research.

Another factor that surfaced in many of our studies and that influenced juror evaluations of witnesses was an interaction between source characteristics of witnesses and the particular mode of presentation. Specifically, some trial participants were evaluated more favorably by jurors when they delivered their testimony live rather than on videotape. Conversely, some trial participants made a more favorable impression on jurors when viewed on videotape rather than live. Identification of these source characteristics would be of theoretical import to communication scholars and of practical utility to legal practitioners faced with decisions concerning the videotaping of witnesses' testimony.

Even though our research has demonstrated that jurors sometimes discuss inadmissible material after being instructed to disregard it, we did not discover any significant effects of this information upon verdict outcomes. This failure to identify a relationship between inadmissible materials and trial verdicts provides evidence for two competing conclusions. Proponents of the medium could use this finding to argue for the expanded use of videotape to ensure jurors are not exposed to inadmissible materials. The finding could also be used by individuals opposed to wider use of videotape to counter such an argument — if inadmissible material has no effect upon verdict oucomes, there is no need to use videotape and edit it out.

We are confident that the presence of typical, mundane inadmissible materials has little effect on jurors' decisions; however, extremely startling or damaging instances of inadmissible testimony may have a noticeable influence on jurors. Moreover, there may be differences that accrue from the introduction of varying amounts of inadmissible materials — this is possible given the results of the second study discussed in Chapter 5. Two lines of related research are suggested by these findings. First, additional research concerning the relationship between the introduction of varying *amounts* of inadmissible materials and verdict outcomes is warranted; second, the effects of damaging instances of inadmissible materials upon jury decisions merit further research attention.

Our findings indicate that passive message recipients, such as jurors, are unable to detect deceptive testimony with much better than chance accuracy. You may recall that the deception studies involved only a direct examination of individuals who were either lying or telling the truth and that the studies were executed apart from the courtroom environment. As was discussed earlier, it seems reasonable to assume that persons, whether in or out of court, exhibit similar nonverbal behaviors when lying. We acknowledged, however, that the intensity of nonverbal cues may vary markedly given widely varying situations and widely varying consequences if lying is detected. Stated differently, there is no reason to believe the nonverbal behaviors exhibited while lying in the studies discussed in Chapter 7 would differ in kind from those exhibited by perjurors during a trial. On the other hand, the manifestations of these behaviors may have been less intense and more difficult to detect.

The next logical step in this area of research is to conduct similar studies within the context of a trial. Jurors should be exposed to perjurors who are subjected to both direct and cross-examination to determine if this aspect of the trial process enhances the possibility of identifying deceitful testimony. More specifically, the intensity of nonverbal behaviors associated with lying might increase and become more visible as a function of being cross-examined. Of course, this possibility presupposes the existence of a set of negative consequences for being detected. Even though the development of research procedures for completing this study would be tricky, they can be devised.

A final area of video research that needs considerably more attention concerns the effects of various production techniques upon juror responses. We examined a limited number of the techniques that could be used when videotaping depositions or trials. Possibly, variations in the camera angles used to tape material, camera panning, zooming of lenses, special effects, and lighting — to name but a few techniques not examined in our research — could influence juror information processing and decision-making. The use of these production techniques, as well as others, should be carefully evaluated.

## SUMMING UP

Considered as a whole, the findings from the studies discussed fail to indicate that the use of videotaped trial materials produces any deleterious effects on juror response. Obviously, however, the issues we have examined constitute but one aspect of the numerous political, economic, social, and legal considerations that impinge upon the decision of whether to make wider use of videotaped court materials. Hopefully, our research will contribute to a more informed overall view of this complex policy question. Having endorsed this relatively modest objective, we turn off our cameras and rest our case.

# REFERENCES

ARMSTRONG, J. J. (1976) "The criminal videotape trial: serious constitutional questions." *Oregon Law Review* 55: 567-585.

BARON, R. S., BARON, P. H. and MILLER, N. (1973) "The relation between distraction and persuasion." *Psychological Bulletin* 80: 310-323.

BERLO, D. and LEMERT, J. (1961) "A factor analytic study of the dimensions of source credibility." Presented at the Annual Convention of the Speech Association of America, New York, December.

———, and MERTZ, R. M. (1969-1970) "Dimensions for evaluating the acceptability of message sources." *Public Opinion Quarterly* 30: 563-576.

BERMANT, G., CHAPPELL, D., CROCKETT, G. T., JACOUBOVITCH, M. D. and McGUIRE, M. (1975) "Juror responses to prerecorded videotape trial presentations in California and Ohio." *Hastings Law Journal* 26: 975-995.

BERMANT, G., McGUIRE, M., McKINLEY, W. and SALO, C. (1974) "The logic of simulation in jury research." *Criminal Justice and Behavior* 1: 224-233.

BERSCHEID, E. and WALSTER, E. H. (1969) *Interpersonal Attraction*. Reading, MA: Addison-Wesley.

BOULDING, K. E. (1975) "Truth or power." *Science* 190: 423.

BRAKEL, S. J. (1975) "Videotape in trial proceedings: a technological obsession?" *American Bar Association Journal* 61: 956-959.

BRANDT, D. R. (1976) "Listener propensity to counterargue, distraction, and resistance to persuasion." Presented at the Annual Convention of the International Communication Association, Portland, OR, April.

BREITROSE, H. S. (1966) The Effects of Distraction in Attentuating Counterarguments. Ph.D. dissertation, Stanford University.

BROEDER, D. W. (1959) "The University of Chicago jury project." *Nebraska Law Review* 38: 744-760.

BROWN, J. S. (1960) *The Motivation of Behavior*. New York: McGraw-Hill.

BRUNSWIK, E. (1947) *Systematic and Representative Design of Psychological Experiments with Results in Physical and Social Perception*. Berkeley: Univ. of California Press.

BURGER, W. E. (1977) "How to break logjam in courts." *U.S. News and World Report*. December 19: 21-27.

BYRNE, D., LONDON, O. and REEVES, K. (1968) "The effects of physical attractiveness, sex, and attitude similarity on interpersonal attraction." *Journal of Personality* 36: 259-271.

COLASANTO, D. and SANDERS, J. (1976) "From laboratory to juryroom: a review of experiments on jury decision-making." CRSO Working Paper No. 136 (July).

COHEN, J. (1969) *Statistical Power Analysis for the Behavioral Sciences*. New York: Academic Press.

COOK, M. (1969) "Anxiety, speech disturbances, and speech rate." *British Journal of Social and Clinical Psychology* 8: 13-21.

COOPER, L. (1932) *The Rhetoric of Aristotle*. New York: Appleton-Century-Crofts.

CORSI, J. R. (1978) "Concept papers: fair hearing project, the University of New Mexico school of law." Manuscript, University of New Mexico.

CRONBACH, L. J. (1951) "Coefficient alpha and the internal structure of tests." *Psychometrika* 16: 297-334.

DANOWSKI, J. (1974) "Organizing and communicating," in J. Shubert (ed.) *Human Communication: Concepts, Principles and Skills.* East Lansing, MI: Michigan State University (HI-H39).

DIBNER, A. (1956) "Cue-counting: a measure of anxiety in interviews." *Journal of Consulting Psychology* 20: 475-478.

DION, K. (1972) "Physical attractiveness and evaluation of children's transgressions." *Journal of Personality and Social Psychology* 24: 207-213.

———, BERSCHEID, E. and WALSTER, E. (1972) "What is beautiful is good." *Journal of Personality and Social Psychology* 24: 285-290.

DITTMAN, A. T. and LLEWELLYN, L. G. (1968) "Relationships between vocalizations and head nods as listener responses." *Journal of Personality and Social Psychology* 11: 98-106.

DORRIS, J. W. (1967) "Persuasion as a function of distraction and counterarguing." Manuscript, University of California at Los Angeles.

EDWARDS, A. L. (1960) *Experimental Design in Psychological Research.* New York: Holt, Rinehart & Winston.

EFRAN, M. E. (1974) "The effect of physical appearance on the judgment of guilt, interpersonal attraction, and severity of recommended punishment in a simulated jury task." *Journal of Research in Personality* 8: 45-54.

EKMAN, P. and FRIESEN, W. V. (1974) "Detecting deception from the body and face." *Journal of Personality and Social Psychology* 29: 288-298.

———, (1969) "Nonverbal leakage and clues to deception." *Psychiatry* 63: 88-106.

ELIOT, W. A., COLEMAN, G. C., PFEFFERKORN, R. G., SIEGEL, L. G., STINE, L. L. and WITTER, A. E. (1976) The Video Telephone in Criminal Justice: The Phoenix Project, Vol. 1: Summary of Applications and Findings. MITRE technical report MTR-7328.

EXLINE, R. V., THIBAUT, J., HICKEY, G. B. and GUMPERT, P. (1970) "Visual interaction in relation to Machiavellianism and an unethical act," pp. 53-75 in R. Christie and F. L. Geis (eds.) *Studies in Machiavellianism.* New York: Academic Press.

FAY, P. J. and MIDDLETON, W. C. (1941) "The ability to judge truthtelling, or lying, from the voice as transmitted over a public address system." *Journal of General Psychology* 24: 211-215.

FESTINGER, L. and MACCOBY N. (1964) "On resistance to persuasive communications." *Journal of Abnormal and Social Psychology* 68: 359-366.

FONTES, N. E., MILLER, G. R. and SUNNAFRANK, M. (1977) "Is justice blind? some possible effects of defendant attractiveness on juridic judgments." *The Metropolitan Washington Communication Association Encoder* 5: 1-20.

FREEDMAN, J. L. (1969) "Role playing: psychology by consensus." *Journal of Personality and Social Psychology* 13: 107-114.

———, and SEARS, D. O. (1965) "Warning, distraction, and resistance to influence." *Journal of Personality and Social Psychology* 1: 262-266.

GARDNER, D. M. (1966) "The effect of divided attention on attitude change induced by a persuasive marketing communication," pp. 523-540 in R. M. Haas (ed.) *Science, Technology and Marketing.* Chicago: American Marketing Association.

GREENBERG, B. S. and ROLOFF, M. E. (1974) "Mass media credibility: research results and critical issues." *ANPA News Research Center Report of Surveys* 6: 3-46.

HAALAND, G. A. and VENKATESAN, M. (1968) "Resistance to persuasive communications: an examination of the distraction hypothesis." *Journal of Personality and Social Psychology* 9: 167-170.

HARRISON, R. P. (1974) *Beyond Words: An Introduction to Nonverbal Communication.* Englewood Cliffs, NJ: Prentice-Hall.

HOFFMAN, H. M. and BRODLEY, J. (1952) "Jurors on trial." *Missouri Law Review* 17: 235-251.

KASL, S. and MAHL, G. (1965) "The relationship of disturbances and hesitations in spontaneous speech to anxiety." *Journal of Personality and Social Psychology* 1: 425-433.

KATZMAN, N. I. (1971) "Violence and color television: what children of different ages learn." Manuscript, Michigan State University.

KEATING, J. P. and BROCK T. C. (1974) "Acceptance of persuasion and the inhibition to counterargumentation under various distraction tasks." *Journal of Experimental Social Psychology* 10: 301-309.

KEPPELL, G. (1973) *Design and Analysis: A Researcher's Handbook.* Englewood Cliffs, NJ: Prentice-Hall.

KESSLER, J. B. (1975) "The social psychology of jury deliberations," pp. 67-93 in R. J. Simon (ed.) *The Jury System in America: A Critical Overview.* Beverly Hills: Sage Publications.

KLINE, F. G. and JESS, P. H. (1966) "Prejudicial publicity: its effect on law school mock juries." *Journalism Quarterly* 43: 113-116.

KNAPP, M. L., HART, R. P. and DENNIS, H. S. (1974) "An exploration of deception as a communication construct." *Human Communication Research* 1: 15-29.

KRAUSE, M. and PILISUK, M. (1961) "Anxiety in verbal behavior: a validation study." *Journal of Consulting Psychology* 25: 414-419.

KRIMERMAN, L. I. (1969) *The Nature and Scope of Social Science: A Criticial Anthology.* New York: Appleton-Century-Crofts.

KUMATA, H. (1960) "Two studies in classroom teaching," pp. 151-157 in W. Schramm (ed.) *The Impact of Educational Television.* Urbana: Univ. of Illinois Press.

*Lansing State Journal* (1975) "Jury duty? good time to deal out the cards." June 29, B-1.

LAZARSFELD, P. F. and MERTON, R. K. (1952) "Transmitting influence through mass communications," pp. 95-118 in G. E. Swanson, *et al.* (eds.) *Readings in Social Psychology.* Ann Arbor, MI: Society for the Psychological Study of Social Issues.

LINDQUIST, E. F. (1953) *Design and Analysis of Experiments in Psychology and Education.* Boston: Houghton Mifflin.

LUND, F. H. (1925) "The psychology of belief: IV. the law of primacy in persuasion." *Journal of Abnormal and Social Psychology* 20: 183-191.

MAIER, N. (1965) "Sensitivity to attempts at deception in an interview situation."
   *Personnel Psychology* 19: 55-65.
————, and THURBER, J. (1968) "Accuracy of judgments of deception when an interview is watched, heard, and read." *Personnel Psychology* 21: 23-30.
MADSEN, R. (1973) *The Impact of Film.* New York: Macmillan.
McCAIN, T., CHILBERG, J. and WAKSHLAG, J. (1977) "The effect of camera
   angle on source credibility and attraction." *Journal of Broadcasting* 21: 35-46.
McCAIN, T. and DIVERS, L. (1973) "The effect of body type and camera shot on
   interpersonal attraction and source credibility." Presented at the Annual Convention of the Speech Communication Association, New York, December.
McCAIN, T. and REPENSKY, G. (1972) "The effect of camera shot on interpersonal
   attraction for comedy performers." Presented at the Annual Convention of the
   Speech Communication Association, Chicago, December.
McCAIN, T. and WAKSHLAG, J. (1974) "The effect of camera angle and image size
   on source credibility and interpersonal attraction." Presented at the Annual Convention of the International Communication Association, New Orleans, April.
McCROSKEY, J. C. (1977) "Oral communication apprehension: a summary of recent
   theory and research." *Human Communication Research* 4: 78-96.
————, (1966) "Scales for the measurement of ethos." *Speech Monographs* 33: 65-72.
———— and MEHRLEY, R. S. (1969) "The effects of disorganization and nonfluency
   on attitude change and source credibility." *Speech Monographs* 36: 13-21.
McCRYSTAL, J. L. (1977) "The promise of prerecorded videotape trials." *American
   Bar Association Journal* 63: 977-979.
McGUIRE, W. J. (1969) "The nature of attitudes and attitude change," pp. 136-314
   in G. Lindzey and E. Aronson (eds.) *Handbook of Social Psychology*, Vol. 3.
   Reading, MA: Addison-Wesley.
McLUHAN, M. (1964) *Understanding Media: The Extensions of Man.* New York:
   McGraw-Hill.
MEHRABIAN, A. (1969) "Methods and designs: some referents and measures of
   nonverbal behavior." *Behavior Research Methods and Instrumentation* 1: 203-207.
————, (1971a) "Nonverbal betrayal of feelings." *Journal of Experimental Research
   in Personality* 5: 64-75.
————, (1971b) *Silent Messages.* Belmont, CA: Wadsworth.
MIHRAM, G. A. (1972) *Simulation: Statistical Foundations and Methodology.* New
   York: Academic Press.
MILLER, G. R., BAUCHNER, J. E., HOCKING, J. E., FONTES, N. E.,
   KAMINSKI, E. P. and BRANDT, D. R. (forthcoming) " '. . . and nothing but the
   truth': how well can observers detect deceptive testimony?" in B. D. Sales (ed.)
   *Perspectives in Law and Psychology*, Vol. 2. New York: Plenum.
MILLER, G. R., BENDER, D. C., BOSTER, F., FLORENCE, B. T., FONTES, N.,
   HOCKING, J. and NICHOLSON, H. (1975) "The effects of videotaped testimony
   in jury trials." *Brigham Young University Law Review* 1975: 331-373.
MILLER, G. R., BENDER, D. C., FLORENCE, B. T. and NICHOLSON, H. E.
   (1974) "Real versus reel: what's the verdict?" *Journal of Communication*
   24: 99-111.
MILLER, G. R. and BOSTER, F. J. (1977) "Three images of the trial: their implications for psychological research," pp. 19-38 in B. D. Sales (ed.) *Psychology in
   the Legal Process.* Jamaica, NY: Spectrum.

MILLER, G. R. and HEWGILL, M. A. (1964) "The effects of variations in nonfluency on audience ratings of source credibility." *Quarterly Journal of Speech* 50: 36-44.

MILLER, N. and CAMPBELL, D. T. (1959) "Recency and primacy in persuasion as a function of the timing of speeches and measurement." *Journal of Abnormal and Social Psychology* 59: 1-9.

MILLER, N. and LEVY, B. H. (1967) "Defaming and agreeing with the communicator as a function of emotional arousal, communication extremity, and evaluation set." *Sociometry* 30: 158-175.

MILLER, N. E. and DOLLARD, J. C. (1971) *Social Learning and Imitation*. New Haven, CT: Yale Univ. Press.

MILLERSON, G. (1964) *The Technique of Television Production*. New York: Hastings House.

MITCHELL, H. E. and BYRNE, D. (1973) "The defendant's dilemma: effects of jurors' attributions and authoritarianism on judicial decisions." *Journal of Personality and Social Psychology* 25: 123-129.

MOORE, C. M. and LANDIS, B. (1975) "Proceedings of a conference on the humanistic aspects of videotaping trials." Manuscript, Kent State University.

NAMBOODIRI, N. K., CARTER, L. F. and BLALOCK, H. M. (1975) *Applied Multivariate Analysis and Experimental Designs*. New York: McGraw-Hill.

NUNNALLY, J. C. (1967) *Psychometric Theory*. New York: McGraw-Hill.

ORNE, M. (1962) "On the social psychology of the psychological experiment: with particular reference to demand characteristics and their implications." *American Psychologist* 17: 776-783.

———, (1959) "The nature of hypnosis: artifact and essence." *Journal of Abnormal and Social Psychology* 58: 277-299.

OSTERHOUSE, R. A. and BROCK, T. C. (1970) "Distraction increases yielding to propaganda by inhibiting counterarguing." *Journal of Personality and Social Psychology* 15: 344-358.

POPE, B. and SIEGMAN, A. (1962) "The effect of therapist verbal activity level and specificity on patient productivity and speech disturbance in the initial interview." *Journal of Consulting Psychology* 26: 489.

REECE, M. M. and WHITMAN, R. N. (1962) "Expressive movements, warmth, and verbal reinforcement." *Journal of Abnormal and Social Psychology* 64: 234-236.

ROSENBLATT, P. C. (1966) "Persuasion as a function of varying amounts of distraction." *Psychonomic Science* 5: 85-86.

RYAN, M. G. (1976) "The influence of teleconferencing media and status on participants' perception of the aestheticism, evaluation, privacy, potency, and activity of the medium." *Human Communication Research* 2: 255-261.

SCHACHTER, S. and SINGER, J. E. (1962) "Cognitive, social and physiological determinants of emotion state." *Psychological Review* 69: 379-399.

SCHAPS, E. and GUEST, L. (1968) "Some pros and cons of color TV." *Journal of Advertising Research* 8: 28-39.

SHAMO, G. W. and MEADOR, L. M. (1969) "The effects of visual distraction upon recall and attitude change." *Journal of Communication* 19: 157-162.

SHELDON, W. (1954) *Atlas of Man: A Guide for Somatyping the Adult Male at All Ages*. New York: Harper & Row.

SCHULMAN, G. (1973) An Experimental Study of the Effects of Receiver Sex, Communicator Sex, and Warning on the Ability of Receivers to Detect Deceptive Communicators. Masters thesis, Purdue University.

SERENO, K. and HAWKINS, G. (1967) "The effects of variations in speakers' nonfluency upon audience ratings of attitude toward the speech topic and speakers' credibility." *Speech Monographs* 34: 58-64.

SIGALL, H. and OSTROVE, N. (1975) "Beautiful but dangerous: effects of offender attractiveness and nature of the crime on juridic judgment." *Journal of Personality and Social Psychology* 31: 410-414.

SILVERMAN, F. and JOHNSTON, R. (1975) "Direct interval-estimation: a ratio scaling method." *Perceptual and Motor Skills* 41: 464-466.

SILVERMAN, I. and REGULA, C. (1968) "Evaluation apprehension, demand characteristics, and the effects of distraction on persuasibility." *Journal of Social Psychology* 75: 273-281.

SIMON, R. J. (1966) "Murder, juries, and the press: does sensational reporting lead to verdicts of guilty?" *Transaction* 3: 40-42.

———, and MAHAN, L. (1971) "Quantifying burdens of proof: a view from the bench, the jury, and the classroom." *Law and Society Review* 5: 319-330.

SUE, S., SMITH, R. E. and CALDWELL, C. (1973) "Effects of inadmissible evidence on the decisions of simulated jurors: a moral dilemma." *Journal of Applied Social Psychology* 3: 345-353.

TIEMENS, R. (1970) "Some relationships of camera angle to communicator credibility." *Journal of Broadcasting* 14: 483-490.

TROVILLO, P. (1939) "A history of lie detection." *Journal of Criminal Law and Criminology* 29: 848-881.

VOHS, J. L. (1964) "An empirical approach to the concept of attention." *Speech Monographs* 31: 355-360.

———, and GARRETT, R. L. (1968) "Resistance to persuasion: an integrative framework." *Public Opinion Quarterly* 32: 445-452.

WANAMAKER, L. (1937) "Trial by jury." *University of Cincinnati Law Review* 11: 191-200.

WELD, H. P. and DANZIG, E. R. (1940) "A study of the way in which a verdict is reached by a jury." *American Journal of Psychology* 53: 518-536.

WIENER, M. and MEHRABIAN, A. (1968) *Language Within Language: Immediacy, a Channel in Verbal Communication.* New York: Appleton-Century-Crofts.

WILLIAMS, R. (1968) "Film shots and expressed interest levels." *Speech Monographs* 35: 166-169.

———, (1965) "On the value of varying TV shots." *Journal of Broadcasting* 9: 33-43.

WINER, B. J. (1971) *Statistical Principles in Experimental Design.* New York: McGraw-Hill.

WURTZEL, A. and DOMINICK, J. (1971-1972) "Evaluation of television drama: interaction of acting styles and shot selection." *Journal of Broadcasting* 16: 103-110.

WYER, R. S. Jr. (1974) *Cognitive Organization and Change: An Information Processing Approach.* New York: John Wiley.

ZIMBARDO, P., MAHL, G. and BARNARD, J. (1963) "The measurement of speech disturbance in anxious children." *Journal of Speech and Hearing Disorders* 28: 362-370.

# ABOUT THE AUTHORS

Gerald R. Miller, who received his B.A. and M.A. in political science from the University of Iowa and his Ph.D. in communication from the same institution, is Professor of Communication at Michigan State University. Dr Miller's major research and teaching areas include communication theory, interpersonal communication, persuasion, and communication in legal settings. He is the editor of Volume 5 of the SAGE Annual Reviews of Communication Research, *Explorations in Interpersonal Communication*, and is presently coediting a second volume in the series dealing with persuasion. He has authored or edited six other books and has written numerous articles for journals of communication, psychology, and law. Professor Miller is a Fellow of the International Communication Association and is presently the President of that association. He is also a member of the Speech Communication Association and the American Psychological Association. His honors include the Speech Communication Association's Annual Award for outstanding scholarly publication in 1967, 1974, and 1976; the Distinguished Faculty Award and the Centennial Review Lectureship from Michigan State University; and a Joint Resolution of Tribute from the Michigan Legislature for the research dealing with courtroom uses of videotape that is reported in this volume.

Norman E. Fontes received his B.A. in Speech Communication from California State University, Northridge and an M.A. and Ph.D. in communication from Michigan State University. His research areas include interpersonal communication and communication in legal settings. He has published book chapters and journal articles concerning persuasion, attitude change, interpersonal communication, and communication in the legal environment.

# Date Due